VARIATIONS IN

BLACK AND WHITE PERCEPTIONS OF THE SOCIAL ENVIRONMENT

Variations in
Black and White Perceptions
of the Social
Environment

EDITED BY

HARRY C. TRIANDIS

SCHOOL OF
CALIFORNIA PROFESSIONAL
PSYCHOLOGY
LOS ANGELES

UNIVERSITY OF ILLINOIS PRESS

Urbana Chicago London

LIBRARY OF CONGRESS CATALOGING IN PUBLICATION DATA

Main entry under title:

Variations in black and white perceptions of the
    social environment.

    Bibliography: p.
    Includes index.
    1. Social perception — Addresses, essays, lectures.
2. Afro-Americans — Psychology — Addresses, essays,
lectures. 3. Communication — Social aspects —
Addresses, essays, lectures. 4. Intercultural
communication — Addresses, essays, lectures.
5. Subculture — Addresses, essays, lectures.
I. Triandis, Harry Charalambos, 1926-
HM132.V37   301.45'1'0420973   75-29056
ISBN 0-252-00515-5

Contents

Introduction

To an observer from another country, the most striking characteristic of domestic American life is the presence of racial conflict. Most countries experience some sort of difficulty in integrating their societies, but the difficulty is generally not so salient as it is in America. The Japanese, for instance, have a certain amount of heterogeneity with respect to Koreans and the Ainu; the Indians have caste and language conflicts; the Belgians and the Irish have language and social class conflicts respectively, although the latter is presented as a conflict of religion. But many of these conflicts are not as visible as the American, although some, like the Irish, are very visible indeed.

Economic, social, and historical roots can be found in most of these conflicts. This is also the case with the American scene, in which ethnic conflict is rooted in many sources (Allport, 1954). One of the several bases of conflict can be found in the differences in the perceptions of the social environment typical of some blacks and whites. They look at the world very differently, and hence they can easily dislike each other, simply because of this fact. There is a good deal of research (e.g., Byrne, 1971) which shows that attitudinal similarity leads to interpersonal attraction. Conversely, dissimilarity leads to disliking. Furthermore, when two people look at their social environment in different ways, they make assumptions concerning the causes of the other's behavior that can lead to further conflict.

To illustrate the subtle ways in which different assumptions can lead to conflict, consider a hypothetical example in which two individuals (let us call them John and George) interact. John is a worker who expects supervisors to be authoritarian; George is a supervisor who has learned about participatory democracy, the need to get workers to contribute their ideas on how jobs should be done, and other aspects of the "human relations" dogma. He believes that a good supervisor encourages his subordinates to participate in decisions, helps them accept responsibility, and gives frequent feedback. Consider a sequence of behavior that might occur between these two men. While the behavior was taking place, each of them had private "interpretations" of what was going on.

Behavior	*Interpretations*
George: How long will it take you to finish this report?	George: I asked him to participate in a decision.
	John: He is the boss; why does he not tell me how long to take?
John: I don't know. How long should it take?	George: He refuses to take responsibility.
	John: I am asking for an order.
George: You are in the best position to estimate the time required.	George: I press him to take responsibility.
	John: I better give him an answer.

John: Ten days.

George knows that the report will take longer, so he says:

George: Take 15 days. O.K.?	George: I offer a contract.
	John: These are my orders — 15 days.

In fact, the report needed much more time — about 30 days of full-time work. So poor John worked day and night, but at the end of the fifteenth day he still needed one more day's work.

Behavior	*Interpretations*
George: Where is the report?	George: I am teaching him to take responsibility for his agreements and to fulfill contracts.
	John: He is asking for the report and expects it to be ready.
John: It will be ready tomorrow.	Both interpret that the report is not ready.

Behavior	*Interpretations*
George: But we had agreed it would be ready today!	George: I am teaching him a useful lesson.
	John: The stupid, incompetent boss! Not only did he give me the *wrong orders,* but he does not even appreciate that I have been working day and night.
John hands in his resignation.	George is surprised and amazed.

In this example the ways of thinking that John and George learned in their subcultures have resulted in specific ways of interpreting what is going on in their interpersonal relationship. Note how their interpretations differ. This is because they use different assumptions about the supervisor-subordinate relationship. We carry such assumptions in our heads, and when we relate to a person who uses different assumptions, we often "misunderstand" him. Such misunderstandings are particularly common when two people have very different cultural backgrounds.

We will use the term "subjective culture" to refer to the way humans who speak a mutually understandable dialect react subjectively to their social environment. The way they attend to cues from the environment, the way they think about "what goes with what," and the way they feel about different aspects of the environment constitute important elements of their subjective culture.

In this book we will discuss the subjective cultures of some samples of blacks and whites. There is good reason to think that these subjective cultures may be very different. Different cultural environments result in different norms (ideas about what is correct behavior in a given social situation), roles (ideas about what is correct behavior for persons holding a particular position in a social group), values (ideas about what states of the world are more desirable than other states), and so on. This happens because people who live together, and talk to each other frequently, develop similar ideas about what is correct behavior or what is desirable. As they converse with people like themselves, they often diverge from other people who speak different languages, live in different places, and with whom they have little contact.

Some of the most important determinants of subjective culture are historical events. The history of race relations in America is too well known to require a review. But it is useful to suggest how it affects the way blacks and whites see their social environment.

The average white American is likely to be relatively well off (statistically this means he has a higher income than most blacks). He feels that this is a land of opportunity, where those who are willing to work hard can have a good life. He feels that he has some say about what is going on in government; the police and other public servants are doing jobs that he might have assigned to them.

Contrast this situation with the black ghetto dweller. He is short of funds; he does not feel a part of the influence structure. He feels that "foreign" invaders, such as the police, social workers, and others, are constantly inspecting him and searching him. He sees his opportunities blocked. He has been hurt too frequently to believe that any white person is really fair — he assumes that almost all whites are prejudiced.

Many white Americans feel that there is something wrong with black ghetto dwellers. But, in fact, anyone placed in that environment would probably develop similar ways of thinking. Clark (1965) has described the objective conditions that characterize the black ghetto: overcrowding, poor housing, high infant mortality, crime, and disease. More than half of the blacks come from the rural South, where discrimination and economic exploitation made their life intolerable. They exchanged one set of undesirable conditions for another, perhaps less undesirable. At any rate, the objective conditions have direct effects at the subjective level — resentment, hostility, despair, apathy, self-depreciation, and sometimes compensatory grandiose behavior. The black ghetto is an island of poverty in a sea of affluence. What is worse, the ghetto blacks can see what is going on outside because television brings the information to them. To compound the problem, the picture of the world that one gets from television is unrealistic. Studies show that about 80% of the "heroes" are professional or middle-class people, living extremely well. When a black looks at his television set and compares his environment to what he sees there, he can only feel resentment.

Many ghetto blacks have no jobs, not because they do not want to work but because there are not enough jobs in this country for people with few skills. Even when they have jobs, they are at the bottom of the prestige ladder — clean-up men, watchmen, garbage collectors, or unskilled workers in assembly lines. The prospects for promotion are essentially zero. The future looks bleak. No wonder, then, that such people often have a low self-esteem (they do not like themselves or think of themselves as particularly important), have short time perspectives (they think of today, not of what will happen next year or in five years), and see only a small connection between what they do and what they get from the environment. The last point means that they do not see a connection between their own actions and success in the world but, rather, believe that most good things in life "just happen" or somebody like the government makes them happen. This is called an external orientation, as opposed to an internal orientation, and can be measured with a scale developed by Rotter (1966).

When you do not have a job, and events in your environment do not happen by the clock, you do not learn to pay attention to them or to regulate your behavior by the clock. The result is that when blacks from the ghetto get jobs, their attendance is not good, they are often late, and they are more likely to quit (Purcell and Cavanagh, 1972). A middle-class person, white or black, is likely to react to such people by characterizing them as unreliable and lazy. Poor attendance is a major cause of dismissal of blacks from industry (APA Symposium, 1969).

Some people say that the ghetto is a jungle. When there are few resources, the competition for them is great. Maruyama (1969) gives an example: A young black returns from his job with $130. A policeman searches him, finds the money, and takes it away, saying: "Punk, I know you couldn't have gotten this money unless you stole it. Well, I'll let you away easy this time, I'll give you $20 back. Make sure you keep your black mouth shut." Under such conditions, is it worthwhile for the black man to go to work? Here is a case in which, no matter how well trained, he cannot cope with his environment unless the environment is changed.

In fact, Jacobs (1966) presents an unbelievable picture of the relationship of ghetto blacks to the government agencies of a major California city, which suggests the need for intensive training of policemen, social workers, and welfare officials in understanding black culture rather than training the blacks. Maruyama (1969) presents several examples of behaviors which are "totally unacceptable" in the white middle-class world which are rationally desirable and obviously functional within the ghetto. For example, violence has a different function in the ghetto from that in middle-class neighborhoods. Consider this excerpt from an interview: "The ghettoes that I have grown up in are, if you did not fight, I mean, you are in trouble, so ah, beat up every day. Your lunch money was taken. Your mother sent you to a store, you know, and you didn't fight, and they knew you wouldn't fight, and the, the money was taken and after money was taken you might get a whip when you get home" (Maruyama, 1968, p. 21).

In such environments violence appears a logically defensible way of life. Similarly, "kindness" is often disfunctional in the ghetto. The logic of the ghetto may not be the same as the logic used by the middle class. For instance, the consequences of prostitution to the middle-class white are more money but also degradation. To the black ghetto member they may include financial independence — hence, self-assertion and self-respect. Maruyama points out that regularly employed women, such as prostitutes, have more prestige in the ghetto than seasonal laborers. Thus a pimp, who has some control over prostitutes, may gain status by accepting such an occupation.

In such situations it is not surprising that people do not trust each other much. It should be obvious that when resources are few, a person cannot afford to trust others. For example, if going to work involves getting a babysitter, and the babysitter eats the food available in the house, one may have to do without food. In short, the babysitter cannot be trusted. Friends in the ghetto can be severe burdens. If they get into trouble they may require your help, but if you help them you will not have enough for yourself. The lack of resources leads to rare interpersonal reinforcement by means of material exchanges. The high frequency of crime and interpersonal exploitation makes trust responses disfunctional. Certain black groups, such as the Panthers, have developed self-protective norms which permit relatively more trust within the group, but in general one cannot trust another. (See Cleaver in *The Black Panther*, August 16, 1969.)

Research evidence seems consistent with these observations. For example, Erskine (1969) reports the results of a poll (NORC, February, 1964) which asked national samples: "Do you think most people can be trusted?" The national total was 77% "Yes," 21% "No"; the corresponding black percentages were 59 and 40. Suspicion seems characteristic of urban populations with an agrarian background, such as the Greeks (Triandis and Vassiliou, 1967b), the southern Italians (Banfield, 1958), and peasant people around the world (Foster, 1965). Such people, according to Foster, develop the idea that good is limited. If something good happens to another person, it is at your own expense.

This idea of "limited good" may be found in rural environments because there good flows from the earth. If you have a large piece of land you are wealthy, while if you have a small piece you may have trouble surviving. When something good happens to another, it means that he acquired more land, which might well be your land. So good events for others might be bad events for you. This is technically called a "zero-sum situation," because the values of the exchange to you and the other sum to zero. The same thing happens when you bargain: If the seller gets 10 cents more, the buyer has 10 cents less; the sum is zero.

It could be, then, that the lack of trust found in the ghetto occurs because of the rural background of most of its residents. However, the chances are that the highly competitive situation which one finds in places with limited resources accentuates the tendency to think in zero-sum terms. In any case, the black ghetto is characterized by low trust, high suspicion, hostility, and competition, and a good deal of "rapping" (Kochman, 1969).

In this book we will examine the extent to which the subjective cultures of the ghetto, as described above, can be found among other kinds of blacks. Is there a black subjective culture? Is the ghetto black subjective culture general or confined to the ghetto?

We were also particularly interested in another question. While many ghetto blacks are poor, they are in absolute numbers less numerous than the white poor. The so-called hardcore unemployed — people with few skills, looking for a job for a long time, and unable to find one — are not all black; in fact, most of them are white. Do the hardcore blacks[1] and whites share any aspect of subjective culture? After all, they both face objectively similar conditions — poverty.

The motivation for the studies to be reported in this book was to

[1] By the term "hardcore blacks" we refer to those individuals with a history of unemployment who were unemployed at the time of the study, were looking for a job, and were unable to find one. The definition we gave to the interviewers conformed with the definition of the Office of Economic Opportunity.

learn about the generality of the ways of thinking found in the black ghetto and to develop a map of this way of thinking which could be compared with the corresponding map of middle-class whites. The idea is that if we teach whites to understand the way of thinking of blacks, they will be able to get along with them better.

This is particularly important in getting jobs for blacks. Industry has programs of black employment. Between 1968 and 1970 more than 400,000 blacks were hired with the help of the National Alliance of Businessmen. But 47% of these blacks quit their jobs within the first six months of employment (Goodale, 1973, p. 2). It is a reasonable guess that quitting is associated with the extent to which the blacks feel unwelcome in white industry. One of the major persons who can make them feel "at home" is the foreman. We thought, then, of developing training programs to help the foreman in white industry understand the point of view of black workers. This we have done. We also developed programs to teach black workers about conditions in industry and the kind of behavior that is expected of them if they are going to feel comfortable there. In order to develop such training programs, we had to know precisely how blacks and whites think about interpersonal relations. To do this, we did the studies reported in this book.

For whom is this book written? We want it to be accessible to any intelligent layman, particularly to undergraduates in any of the social sciences. To make it accessible to such a wide audience, we had to use nontechnical language. But we had a problem: most of the analyses of the data used very complicated statistical procedures. How can we present them here and still hope that a person without advanced training in statistics will be able to understand the results of our studies? We tried our best to explain the statistical procedures so that a person without statistical background can at least get a feel for what we did and can understand the tables of results.

We thought that being able to look at these tables might be particularly valuable because we have not "milked" the data completely dry of their implications. On the contrary, we skimmed the most important findings. So an undergraduate looking for a paper topic for a social science course might well find it possible to study our tables, extract information from here and there, plot the data on different kinds of graphs, and come up with an interesting paper. The fact that we present a very rich array of data of all sorts should make his task most interesting.

The printing of tables is an extremely expensive aspect of any book. Our compromise consists of presenting the tables in microfiche. At the end of the book we present a list of the tables that will be found in the microfiche folder. These are the bases of the arguments made in the text. Thus a student wishing to use our tables will need to go to a library where microfiche readers are available.

However, the data are also interesting to the specialist. A specialist might also be interested in more details of why we did a particular analysis or how and precisely what statistical results we did obtain. We assume that the specialist will be willing to look for such details in the footnotes and in Chapter 5. Many readers may well ignore these, but the specialist might find them the most interesting parts of the book.

The data presented in this book can help a person understand some aspects of the way of thinking of blacks and whites. Such ways of thinking have implications for interpersonal behavior. The problem is general, since two people from different cultures are likely to have more trouble getting along than two people from the same culture. In order to place the data in context, we begin the book with a chapter on interpersonal behavior across cultures. We discuss in that chapter what aspects of the interpersonal relationship are important, how we can study these aspects, and what determines how people behave in social settings. From this general discussion we might learn what aspects of subjective culture are most helpful in understanding interpersonal relationships. This suggests what specific aspects of black and white subjective cultures we should study. In the next chapter we discuss how we can train people from one culture to understand the point of view of people from another culture, using a training approach which is called the "culture assimilator." We show how different parts of the culture assimilator train a person in the different skills needed to get along with persons from another culture.

These two chapters, then, set the broad stage, explaining both how to approach the study of subjective culture and what to do with the information one gets from such a study. The third chapter introduces the study; the fourth presents white and black differences in the meaning of words. The fifth goes into the method used to collect the data reported in the next two chapters. Chapter 8 presents some examples of the way the information presented in Chapters 6 and 7 can be used to train people to interact more effectively with members of the black community. The final chapter summarizes our findings and discusses some of their implications.

The work on this book, with the exception of Chapter 4 by Landis et al., was supported by a research grant to H. C. Triandis (no. 15-P-55175/5 from the Social and Rehabilitation Service of the Department of Health, Education and Welfare). The work reported in Chapter 4 was supported by ETS Grant no. 865-12 to D. Landis, NSF and NIMH grants to C. E. Osgood (data analysis), and NSF Grant no. GS30952X to Landis.

CHAPTER ONE

Interpersonal Behavior across Cultures

H . C . T R I A N D I S

Culture has been defined by some anthropologists (e.g., Herskovits, 1955) as the man-made part of the human environment. This includes not only artifacts but also laws, myths, and special ways of thinking about the social environment. Subjective culture is a cultural group's characteristic way of viewing the man-made part of the environment. It is the reaction of a homogeneous group of people to the social environment. By "cultural group" we mean a homogeneous group of people who speak a mutually understandable dialect. Thus a group of physicians discussing a medical problem would, by this definition, constitute a cultural group.

Granted that this is an unusual definition of a cultural group, we believe it is defensible on the grounds that we should not assume that people react to their social environment homogeneously until we have empirical proof. To say that Americans view their social environment in a particular way is often absurd, since the within-group variance is so great as to make the statement meaningless. This is not to say that there are no specific issues on which homogeneity of views might exist. There are, undoubtedly, many cultural truisms which are not debated by members of any cultural group, and hence we might find large groups who have similar reactions to these truisms. However, until we have some empirical proof of homogeneity, it is best to assume that people who differ in race, sex, age, nationality, religion, social class, occupation, language, or geographical environment might have different subjective cultures.

Subjective cultures differ because people who interact with similar others develop consensus on how to look at the world. Since humans interact with a very small sample of other humans, they frequently develop unique ways of viewing their environments which differ from the views of most other humans. When two persons who have different subjective cultures come together to do something, it is likely that they will have difficulties in agreeing on how to do it. There are innumerable examples of circumstances when subjective cultures differ. To sketch the extent of the problem, we will mention a few.

Interracial difficulties are common not only in the United States but also in many other parts of the world. Sometimes, as in Africa, they are very serious, and sometimes, as in Japan or Brazil, they are of minor significance. But, nevertheless, they are important in most parts of the world. In many cases they are correlated with differences in social class; sometimes there are no members of certain racial groups in certain occupations.

The women's liberation movement has emphasized the division of points of view among men and women in some parts of the world. The generation gap illustrates difficulties owing to differences in subjective culture associated with age. Nationalism and international conflict are so well known that they only need to be mentioned. Religious strife was historically of major significance in Europe, where the Thirty Years' and Hundred Years' wars were, in part, explained by differences in religious orientation. Linguistic strife can be seen in several countries, e.g., Belgium and India, and is often associated with local nationalism.

In all these examples there are some realistic bases of conflict. For example, there is some goal that one group tries to reach which is very different from the goal of another group. Consider a labor-management dispute. If labor is asking for a wage increase of 50 cents an hour, this means that management would have to pay 50 cents more an hour, if it were to agree. This is a zero-sum situation, since what is won and lost sums to zero. This *is* realistic conflict. But there are many situations in which conflict is due to misunderstandings, wrong assumptions, and differences in subjective culture that are unrelated to the actual situation. The present chapter will be concerned with the latter type of conflict.

Granted that much conflict is realistic. There are major problems of exploitation of one human by another all around the world; there is much zero-sum conflict; it is true that some people have access to large resources while others have no such access. These problems cannot be handled effectively by psychologists. Often the solution may require a revolution, or economic reforms, or new laws. Psychologists, on the other hand, can deal with situations in which people perceive the world differently although there is no compelling natural cause requiring them to do so. For example, people may perceive a relationship as zero-sum when in fact it can be rearranged to the benefit of both parties.

In short, in this chapter we will examine situations in which psychological factors divide two or more individuals and make it difficult for them to reach an effective and cooperative relationship, when they both desire to do so.

EXAMPLES OF INTERCULTURAL DIFFICULTIES

In the Introduction we presented an example of intercultural difficulties. We could present many more but will limit our presentation to just a few.

A common problem in cross-cultural encounters involves the expectations that people bring to social situations. For example, in most cultures servants do most of the domestic tasks, including the cleaning of shoes. However, in the United States cleaning ladies typically do not clean shoes. Now if a person from another culture visits the U.S. and asks an American cleaning lady to clean his shoes, she is likely to perceive his request as inappropriate. The crucial question is, however, what attributions she makes concerning his behavior. If she attributes it to "ignorance of American customs," she may not be upset. On the other hand, if she attributes it to a personality syndrome (i.e., the visitor is domineering or obnoxious), there will be damage to the interpersonal relationship.

More subtle difficulties arise when a person from another culture expects respect to be given to him because of his age, profession, or other status, and expects this respect to be manifested in "different speech" — soft, polite, hesitant. An exuberant American is likely to be loud and, what is worse, critical, when the visitor deviates from his expectations. In such a case the damage to the relationship can be irreparable, if the person comes from a culture where superiors have been trained never to forget the "insubordination" of their subordinates.

Note that both of the above examples can be analyzed in terms of behaviors appropriate for a role. In the first the visitor assumes that his role (master to servant) allows him to ask the cleaning lady to clean his shoes; but the American cleaning lady to guest of the household role is incompatible with this behavior. In the second example the old to young man role, or the expert to apprentice role, leads the visitor to expect a particular quality in the interaction. When this is violated, it produces problems.

Many of these problems are not immediately visible, because relations across cultures are often formal, polite, and remote. Nevertheless, the cooperation pattern between individuals does suffer, and the relations are not as effective as they might have been without these "unpleasant incidents." Any one of these incidents does not damage a relationship permanently, but a series of them often does, and one of the most common responses is flight. The disgusted visitor leaves and never returns. Understanding these human interactions requires closer analysis.

The More Detailed Analysis

A major problem in intercultural behavior is that each interactor is unable to control the behavior of the other. He cannot do so because he does not understand the causes of the other's behavior. He does not know, for example, how the other analyzes his social environment and what constitutes a reward for the other. In short, he makes wrong attributions concerning the behavior of the other.

Effective intercultural relations require "isomorphic attributions." Isomorphic attributions correspond to this idea: "If I had been raised in that culture and had had the kinds of experiences that he has had, I would do exactly what he did." One could substitute "valid" or "correct" for "isomorphic," but we prefer a term that has no surplus meaning for the reader. Since a person sees his own behavior as controlled by external factors (Jones and Nisbett, 1971), and usually reasonable as well as desirable, isomorphic attributions result in a positive evaluation of the other.

Interpersonal competence means, in part, that a person is able to reward the other. In order for a person to reward another, he needs to control resources. He also needs to know what is rewarding to the other. In intercultural encounters part of the difficulty stems from ig-

norance of what is rewarding to the other. One knows what is rewarding to the other, in part, if one knows his subjective culture.

In intercultural situations we do not know the right cues indicating
what is rewarding to another person. For example, in Egypt one might
express approval of the food served by a host by belching. This is a
cue which can be seen as a direct compliment. In other cultures, of
course, the same behavior is most impolite. There are many ways one
can reward another person. One can show his affection, or admiration,
or do something helpful for him, or give him some useful information
or some money or a gift. Each of these exchanges is an example of a
general class of human exchanges discussed by Foa (1971).

Foa has described how six kinds of exchanges differ from each other.
People exchange Love, Status, Services, Information, Money, and
Goods, as mentioned in the above example. But the exchanges differ
qualitatively, so that they can be represented in a circular pattern, as
shown below:

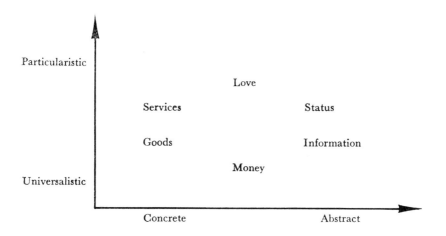

Foa argues that Love is closer to Status than it is to Money, because
the exchanges shown above differ in two qualities. Love, Services, and
Status are more particularistic in the sense that you exchange them with
particular individuals and it makes a great deal of difference with
whom you exchange. Goods and Money can be exchanged with almost
anybody. A person who sells stock at the stock exchange, for instance,
may not even know to whom he is selling it. The second quality is that

Services and Goods are more concrete — they can be seen. Status and Information are more abstract — they cannot be touched. Furthermore, particularistic exchanges require much time, while universalistic exchanges require little time. You can write a check for a million dollars (if you have it) in less than a minute, but you cannot make love in that little time! Because the exchanges differ in quality as shown in the diagram above, it is more appropriate to exchange one of them with itself — return Love when you receive Love — or one of its neighbors. When you exchange at a great distance across the circle, you often run into trouble or do something that is not considered correct. For example, when you exchange Money for Love, that is prostitution; if you offer Money to a hostess after a dinner, she would be offended.

Cultures differ in the kinds of differentiations they make. It is well known, for instance, that different languages have many or few words for particular parts of the environment. A well-known example is the number of words for different kinds of snow found among the Eskimo, the 900 words that have something to do with camels found in Arabic, and the huge number of words that refer to cars found among Americans. What this means is that people pay differential attention to different aspects of the environment. When there is a word for some aspect of the environment, it is possible to refer to it more efficiently, to learn new things about it more quickly, and to remember those things better and longer (for a review, see Triandis, 1964a).

Usually, when it helps to make a particular differentiation, people in the culture will make it. This is called "functionalism" — when something is functional, one does it. Since dealing with some aspects of the environment but not others is often functional, cultures develop different ways of cutting the pie of experience.

For example, some cultures differentiate among people in more complex ways than others. In some places people are either "relatives and friends" or "enemies." That is a simple two-category break. In other places people use dozens of cues to discriminate among people. They do so with different degrees of refinement with respect to each of the exchanges described by Foa. They may see a large or no difference among people on the status dimension, or may give to some people all the information known about a topic but not give it to others; the differentiations can be small or large. In Austria they still use many titles, and a Herr Professor Dr. Dr. (with two doctorates) has more prestige than a professor with only one. In America a person with two or even ten doctorates is not likely to receive more respect *because of* the number of doctorates than a person with only one doctorate. In short, there is less discrimination (fine cutting of the dimension) here on the status dimension.

People can also show much or little differentiation of time. In some cultures every five-minute period is a distinct entity. In others a one-day period is good enough. If you are invited to dinner in America or Japan, you are expected to appear (depending on the size of the city) between 15 and 30 minutes of the appointed time. In a traditional Greek village within three hours of the approximate time of day is sufficient. It is likely that in invitations issued across remote African villages the guests are expected to be there "within a day."

A person who makes a refined differentiation in a particular domain of the environment will often find it difficult to deal with a person who makes no such differentiations, and vice versa. For example, if a person expects to buy a Rolls Royce for the same price as a VW, on the grounds that they are both "cars," he is likely to find it difficult to interact with automobile salesmen. The same problem presents itself in interpersonal exchanges when a person who makes a fine differentiation on a particular exchange deals with a person who makes only a very rough differentiation.

Cultures differ in many ways, but their degree of complexity is one of the most important ones. That is, if you look at all the cultures of the world, you find many types of differences but the degree of differentiation is *the* major dimension of difference (Lomax and Berkowitz, 1972). The very simple cultures (gathering and fishing) and the very complex (highly industrial) have relatively simple family structures. At an intermediate level of complexity one finds the more complex family structures (Blumberg and Winch, 1972). A person who is used to such complex family structures, with extended families, can again have interpersonal difficulties when dealing with a person who does not pay attention to such complexities in his family.

We can, then, consider two types of difficulties. One is the interpersonal difficulty which is traceable to differences in subjective culture;

the other is the type of difficulty which is traceable to the degree of differentiation of various cognitive structures. There is much evidence that the greater the proportion of similar attitudes between two people, the more attracted they are to each other (Byrne, 1969). In a similar way we can conceive that the greater the overlap in the subjective cultures of two people, the greater will be the attraction between them. However, some elements of subjective culture are more general and have implications about a lot of behaviors, while other elements are more specific (Triandis, 1972). Triandis, Weldon, and Feldman (1974) considered four levels of abstraction. At the highest level are values, next norms, then roles, and finally, the least abstract, facilities. If two individuals disagree on values, this has implications about many of their behaviors. For instance, if they disagree on equality or cleanliness or efficiency, with one person saying that one of these concepts is highly desirable and the other saying that it is undesirable, they are disagreeing on many specific elements of subjective culture. In the case of norms, if two individuals disagree on whether there should be absolute equality between the sexes, or on whether the dishes should be washed after every meal, or on whether jobs should be designed so that they are done most efficiently or in the way that is most agreeable to the worker, the disagreement is clearly at a lower level of abstraction because such disagreements do not preclude agreement about other issues. While the two might disagree on equality between the sexes, they may agree about equality between the races, or that the house should be cleaned every week, or that efficiency is important in designing a lecture for the maximum presentation of different materials in the minimum time. In short, while disagreement on values is general, disagreement on norms is more specific.

Still more specific is disagreement on roles. This type of disagreement concerns *who* is supposed to do what. Finally, disagreement on facilities concerns *how* it is to be done. For instance, two people may disagree on whether the dishes should be washed by the husband or the wife, or with the dishwasher or by hand. It is obvious that such disagreements imply agreement at the higher levels of abstraction, namely that the dishes should be washed and that cleanliness is better than dirtiness.

Triandis, Weldon, and Feldman (1974) presented empirical evidence consistent with the above arguments. They showed that two people who disagree on values are seen as disliking each other and behaving toward each other in the future in ways that are highly negative. The effect is not as strong for disagreements on norms. It is even less strong for roles and least strong for facilities. In short, it appears that all elements of subjective culture are not equally important in producing interpersonal difficulties. Those elements that are most abstract are the ones that produce the most difficulties.

We can summarize the kinds of interpersonal difficulties which are likely to occur when persons from two cultures work together.

First, people might attend to different aspects of the social environment. One person might be "tuned" to look for certain kinds of behaviors which the other person might ignore.

Second, they might use words differently. For example, one person might use the word *bad* to mean bad, while the other might use it to mean good (e.g., a black who says "Baby, you look bad" is paying a compliment).

Third, one person might make refined judgments about a particular dimension, while the other might react to it grossly.

Fourth, the person from one culture might see certain social cues attached to behavior and weigh the importance of the cues in one way, while a person from another culture might use entirely different weights.

Fifth, the two might disagree about elements of subjective culture at different levels of abstraction.

While these types of interpersonal difficulties have been illustrated with some examples above, it is necessary to analyze them in greater detail at this time to see what determines the way two people get along with each other.

Broadly speaking, a person p reacts to another o depending on the nature of three kinds of influences: the characteristics of the other (o), the social situation in which p and o find themselves, and p's "implicit personality theory" (his way of thinking about how human traits are organized and how cues are related to behavior). It should also be clear that p makes many different responses to o. Our analysis will begin with a discussion of the kinds of responses that p makes to o; we will then analyze the characteristics of o which elicit such responses and will then discuss the social situation and the implicit personality theories that p might use in perceiving o.

TYPES OF RESPONSES THAT p MAKES TO o

There are three broad types of responses that p makes:

(1) Attributions — ideas about causes of o's behavior. These can be (a) stereotypes (e.g., all Negroes are lazy), (b) inferences (e.g., he did it because he was pressured by his mother), and (c) interpretations (e.g., he laughed to cover up his embarrassment). (2) Evaluations — affective responses toward o, such as thinking that o is good, valuable, or nice or feeling good at the thought of o. (3) Interpersonal acts — giving and denying Love, Status, Information, Money, Goods, or Services, as described above.

Extensive work has shown that humans make different kinds of interpersonal responses. Such responses fall along different "dimensions." A statistical method called factor analysis has been used extensively to determine what responses people give to hypothetical social situations. These studies have shown that people show Respect (e.g., they say they would admire o's ideas or character), Friendship (e.g., they say they would be partners with o or would gossip with him), Intimacy (e.g., have sexual intercourse with o), Social Distance (e.g., reject o from their club or neighborhood), and Superordination (e.g., criticize o) in the kinds of social situations in which blacks and whites face each other in American social settings (Triandis, 1964b).

Such exchanges involve different mixtures of the basic ingredients found in Foa's system, which we discussed earlier. Respect, for instance, implies giving both Status and a little Love; Friendship means giving both Love and a little Status; Intimacy implies giving Love in highly particularistic situations; Social Distance implies denying Status; Superordination implies denying both Status and Love.

The empirically determined dimensions of social exchange did not include the exchanges of Information, Money, and Goods, because Triandis (1964b) obtained the behaviors which he studied from a content analysis of novels, which typically deal with highly particularistic human relationships. The Foa system is more general.

We conclude, then, that p is likely to make attributions about o, is likely to evaluate o, and is likely to give or deny one or more of the exchanges described by Foa.

THE OTHER AS A STIMULUS

A person sends thousands of cues to his social environment. His height, weight, color, clothes, voice type, walking manner, etc. may or may not be attended to by another depending on the utility of these cues in the particular environment. In many situations, for instance, the nationality of the other may make no difference in the kinds of responses made by p. For example, if p is a professor and o is a student, o's nationality may have nothing to do with whether p will show respect to o. On the other hand, other characteristics may be quite important. For example, in America a person's race is a very important cue. In fact, if we compare race, social class, religion, and nationality as cues, we find that for Americans race is the most important (Triandis and Triandis, 1960, 1962), while for Greeks religion is more important, and for Germans and Japanese social class is more important (Triandis, Davis, and Takezawa, 1965; Triandis and Triandis, 1965).

The cues that p will pay attention to are the ones that (a) are familiar to him, (b) are distinctive, and (c) reduce uncertainty (Gibson, 1969). In America race is a familiar concept, while walking in a jumping manner is not. The result is that an American is more likely to notice another's race than another's style of walking. The distinctiveness of a cue is important, however, since a person who walks in an extremely peculiar manner will be noticed as being an unusual walker. Finally, the extent to which p does not know how to behave toward o and some characteristic of o makes p more sure of how he should behave, determines whether p will notice this characteristic. For example, if p does not know whether to go through a door first or let o go first, he will notice o's sex, age, and other characteristics that might help him decide.

One of the most important aspects of cue utilization in interpersonal situations involves comparisons between the characteristics of p and o. If p is very tall, he might notice o's height. Extreme similarity or dissimilarity in the characteristic makes the characteristic more distinctive. Many other characteristics of o relative to p may add to distinctiveness, such as whether o's status on various dimensions of individual status is consistent (a situation called status congruence), or p and o's statuses are consistent (a situation called status equilibrium). Sampson (1969) has reviewed the relevance of status congruence in interpersonal perception. Interpersonal perception can also be analyzed via equity theory (Adams, 1965; Walster, Berscheid, and Walster, 1973), which deals with the way *p* reacts when *o* has better or worse outcomes than *p* relative to the inputs of each.

THE SOCIAL SITUATION

Broadly speaking, the more similar the goals of *p* and *o,* the more attracted they will be to each other, the more complimentary will be the attributions that they make about each other's behavior, and the more likely it is that they will give interpersonal rewards to each other rather than deny them. Furthermore, the longer the period of time that *p* and *o* have known each other, the more intimate they are likely to be in their exchanges.

However, intimacy does not imply interpersonal attraction. People who have had a long period of acquaintance may behave very negatively to each other. In fact, it is still true that most murders occur among people who have known each other for a long time.

Finally, when one person has more resources than the other, he is likely to receive more Status from the other. In short, the *relative* interpersonal characteristics of *p* and *o* determine the attributions, evaluations, and interpersonal behaviors that are likely to take place between *p* and *o.*

The social situation can influence not only what *p* says to *o* but also the "paralinguistic" aspects of the relationship, such as how much eye contact they have with each other, how close they sit to each other, whether they touch each other frequently, whether they smile at each other, and so on. Argyle and Kendon (1967) have presented an integrated theory of the way the social situation influences such behaviors. Bear (1973) has analyzed paralinguistic behaviors in terms of two dimensions, intimacy and positive versus negative affect, and has developed a model which relates different behaviors, such as the percentage of eye contact, to these two variables.

THE PERCEIVER

The age and culture of the perceiver are important determinants of what he perceives. There is evidence that children perceive the "superficial characteristics" of the other, such as his dress, but as they grow older they pay more attention to his "psychological states." Thus, for instance, children notice dress more than facial expression up to about age seven but then notice facial expression more than dress in making judgments about *o* (Levi-Schoen, 1964).

As already mentioned, different cultural groups pay attention to different characteristics of the other, such as race, age, etc. Triandis (1967) summarized numerous studies showing cultural differences in the degree to which *p*s from different cultures pay attention to various characteristics of *o*s.

Humans hold views concerning how traits go together. For instance, the idea that fat people are jolly is an element of the implicit personality theory of Americans and many other people. Such conceptions obviously influence the way humans react to each other because while the presence of many traits is easily determined objectively, other traits are not observable. If a person connects an easily available trait to another trait, the latter trait will be perceived even when there is no other evidence that *o* has it.

INTERPERSONAL BEHAVIOR

We can distinguish two broad kinds of determinants of human behavior: (a) behavioral intentions and (b) habits. When a person instructs himself to behave in a certain way and he does so, his behavior is under the influence of behavioral intentions. For example, when he says to himself, "I better stop studying and go to the dining room" and then engages in the myriad of micro-acts that take him to the dining room, he behaves under the influence of a behavioral intention. When a behavior has taken place many times, the person often does it without thinking, automatically. Then we can say that the behavior is determined by habit. New and complex behaviors are first under the influence of behavioral intentions, but as they occur more and more frequently, the relative importance of behavioral intentions declines and the relative importance of habit increases. Thus when a person learns a new language, he first consciously imitates his teacher. Later, after a lot of practice, he speaks without thinking about it.

The behavioral intentions of a person are determined by three broad kinds of influences: (1) Social influences — norms (ideas about what is correct behavior for any member of a social group), roles (ideas about what is correct behavior for a person holding a particular position in a social group), interpersonal agreements (e.g., when two people agree to meet at 8 P.M.), general behavioral intentions (e.g., to be cooperative, to be intimate, to be bossy), all of which are in turn directly dependent on the nature of the social situation, as discussed earlier, and his self-concept (e.g., I am the sort of person who does this). (2) P's liking for the behavior — the extent to which he gets a kick from doing it. (3) The perceived consequences of the behavior and the value of these consequences.

The latter influence can be analyzed by looking at the perceived consequences of the behavior and asking, first, how likely it is that the behavior will be followed by the particular consequence and, second, how much "fun" or "trouble" is associated with the particular consequence. Of course, a behavior might have several perceived consequences. Then we must multiply the probability of each of these consequences with its value and sum these several products to get a total index of the third influence.

The details of this way of thinking about human behavior, which is called a paradigm (Kuhn, 1962), can be found in Triandis (1975a and b). It suffices here to say that the paradigm states which concepts (or variables) are important in the study of behavior. As we have seen, they are norms, roles, behavioral intentions, the self-concept, the liking for the behavior, the perceived consequences, and the value of the consequences of the behavior.

In the main chapters of this book we will outline the way blacks and whites of different social classes and ages react to their social environment by presenting studies of some of these concepts. Specifically, we will study an aspect of their attributions (stereotyping), their roles and behavioral intentions, as well as the perceived consequences of particular events. This does not represent a complete study of the subjective culture of blacks and whites. Such a study would have been extremely expensive and beyond current resources. We selected the most promising aspects of subjective culture for our study, guiding our selection with considerations derived from both the paradigm we have just outlined and the advice of experts on intergroup and race relations.

Before turning to the results of the studies, however, we wish to clarify our aims once more by pointing out that we intended to use the material for culture training. Such training, according to the analysis of the Introduction and the present chapter, should accomplish certain goals. We summarize these goals in the next chapter.

SUMMARY

The course of interpersonal interaction is determined by many factors. Among the most important are the rewards, relative to the costs, experienced by each participant. When a person receives valuable resources from another, and when the other's behavior is predictable, the interaction is rewarding. Interactions involving people from different cultures often involve more costs than rewards, because each person is often unable to give rewards to the other, and the behavior of the other is frequently unexpected. Behavior acquires its meaning from the attributions that each makes about the causes of the other's behavior. To make accurate attributions requires knowledge of the way people perceive their social environment, or their subjective culture. When persons with different cultural backgrounds make attributions, they are often inaccurate; the inaccuracy leads to different interpretations of the behavior, with the result that the behavior is often a cost rather than a reward. Also, lack of understanding of the subjective culture of another group results in unexpected interaction, which further deteriorates the relationship. One way to ensure that such deterioration does not occur is to train each person to understand the subjective culture of the other. In the present volume we describe the subjective cultures of blacks and whites in the Midwest. The information was obtained in order to construct training materials that will improve interaction between these groups.

CHAPTER TWO

The Culture Assimilator: An Approach to Cultural Training

H. C. TRIANDIS

In the Introduction we mentioned that intercultural misunderstandings occur for many reasons, one of which is that people make different assumptions concerning the causes of another person's behavior. When they do not know the culture of the other person, they are particularly likely to make mistakes in assigning causes to the other's behavior. In this chapter we will first examine interpersonal behavior across cultures. We will then describe an approach called the culture assimilator which provides training in effective interaction with persons from other cultures.

THEORETICAL ANALYSIS

A major problem in intercultural behavior is that each interactor is unable to control the behavior of the other. He cannot do so because he does not understand the causes of the other's behavior. He does not know, for example, how the other analyzes his social environment and what constitutes a reward for the other. In short, he makes mistaken attributions concerning the behavior of the other.

We have already mentioned that effective intercultural relations require "isomorphic attributions." Recall that isomorphic attributions correspond to the idea: "If I had been raised in that culture and had had the kinds of experiences that he has had, I would do exactly what he did." Isomorphic attributions result in a positive evaluation of the other.

The reader is also reminded that interpersonal competence means, in part, that a person is able to reinforce the other. This can happen only if the actor controls resources. He also needs to know what is reinforcing to the other. In intercultural encounters part of the difficulty stems from ignorance of what is reinforcing to the other. One knows what is reinforcing the other, in part, if one knows his subjective culture.

In intercultural exchanges we often do not know what is reinforcing because we do not know the exact persons, situations, etc. which make an exchange rewarding or unrewarding. The ability to make isomorphic attributions means exactly that — the person can correctly infer what is likely to be reinforcing, to what exent, under what conditions, etc., and hence he is able to reinforce the other.

One great difficulty in intercultural encounters occurs when the member from culture A is used to weak norms and the member from culture B is used to strong norms concerning a particular behavior. Here a person is likely to behave in ways which would be "inexcusable" from the other's perspective. It is thus not only when norms are different that intercultural encounters can lead to interpersonal hostility. When the *strength* of the connections between norms and behavior is not the same, the effects can be just as serious. Norm disagreements, furthermore, are only one element that causes problems.

To summarize, then, effective intercultural behavior requires similar differentiations of the significant aspects of the social situation, accurate knowledge of the way one person differs in his attributions from another, accurate expectations, similar role definitions, and similar strengths in the connections between norms or roles on the one hand and behavior on the other. The interculturally effective individual knows how to analyze the behavior of the other, and he focuses on the rewards and punishments which particular behaviors will provide for others. He attributes such behavior to complex interactions of situational and subjective culture variables rather than merely to the culture of the other.

Triandis (1975a) examined the theoretical bases for intercultural training. Here we present only a summary of his main points. Cultural training should accomplish the following goals.

1. Familiarize the student of culture with the dimensions that make a difference in interpersonal behavior in the other culture. This re-

quires the presentation of situations in which what is likely to happen in the learner's culture differs a good deal from what is likely to happen in the other culture.

2. It should make possible the transfer of learning of the new information concerning what is important in the other culture to new situations. Maximum transfer occurs when the new situations maximally contrast the features of the correct and incorrect discriminations, and when familiar but distinctive features are enhanced. In short, the learner must become familiar with the distinctive features of the other culture and the cues indicating what is important.

3. It should increase isomorphic attributions. This means the learner should make judgments about the causes of the other's behavior that are similar to the judgments made by members of the other's culture. If the paradigm described in the previous chapter is to be useful, it should present the learner with the following kinds of information:

(a) norms for different kinds of situations in the other culture;

(b) role structures, in particular, the way role perceptions differ in his culture and the other's culture;

(c) the way behaviors express general intentions in the other culture (e.g., in Egypt to compliment the host after the dinner, one belches);

(d) the kinds of self-concepts that are frequently found in the other culture;

(e) the kinds of behaviors that are valued and disvalued in the other culture;

(f) the kinds of antecedents and consequents of these behaviors that are frequently conceived in the other culture;

(g) the kinds of differentiations that are common in the other culture among types of people, within and between modes of exchange, as well as across time and place;

(h) the strength of the connections between norms, roles, the self-concept, general intentions, affect toward the behavior, and instrumentality of the behavior in the other culture — i.e., the weights of the determinants of social behavior in that culture;

(i) the amplitude of the responses that people in the other culture generally make in various social situations;

(j) the kinds of reinforcement that people expect in different situations and the appropriateness of the exchange of particular reinforcements (e.g., you can exchange Love for Status but not Money for Love).

4. It should familiarize the learner with typologies of culture and the implications of dealing with persons from a more or less differentiated culture, in particular domains of interpersonal exchange.

A training approach which can accomplish these goals is the "culture assimilator." This form of training, suggested by Stolurow and Osgood, was developed by Fiedler and Triandis in the course of a research project in which these four psychologists collaborated. An account of the first validation studies involving this approach is presented by Fiedler, Mitchell, and Triandis (1971) and Mitchell, Dossett, Fiedler, and Triandis (1972).

DESCRIPTION OF THE ASSIMILATOR

The culture assimilator is a book that consists of several hundred "items." Each item occupies six pages. On page 1 there is a journalistic description of an incident in which people from two cultures had trouble getting along with each other or misunderstood what happened in a particular social encounter. The next page presents four interpretations of what went wrong. These interpretations can be considered causal attributions about the observed behavior. Only one of the four attributions is correct from the perspective of the other culture. Thus, if p, the trainee, is from culture A and o is from culture B, p sees an incident in which somebody like him interacts with somebody like o. There are three attributions of the type that is often given by members of culture A to explain this incident and one attribution of the type given by members of culture B to explain the same incident. The trainee now selects the one attribution which he considers the correct interpretation of what happened in the incident. If he selects the correct one from the point of view of the other culture, he is praised and given some concepts and principles which should help him understand the subjective culture of the people whose culture he is trying to learn. If he is incorrect, he is told to try again and select another answer. An example follows.

Page X-1

Russell is an older white man who has worked on a city street crew for more than 20 years. About three years ago the first blacks were hired.

Russell felt the blacks thought they were better than the whites because the black men would refuse to do some of the dirtier, harder jobs. One day when the crew was supposed to be working on the city sewer lines, the blacks refused to go down into the manhole. Russell confronted the black men directly (rather than complaining to the supervisor) and said, "Do you think you are better than I am? I go down into that hole." One of the black men laughed and went down into the manhole. There were no more problems after that.

Page X-2

Why did the black men decide to "go into the hole?"

1. The supervisor got angry at them and made them do it.
Please go to page X-3
2. Because they decided they weren't better than the whites after all.
Please go to page X-4
3. Because they realized that it was part of the job.
Please go to page X-5
4. They knew that Russell had seniority and could tell them what to do.
Please go to page X-6

Page X-3

You selected 1: The supervisor got angry at them and made them do it.

This is not the correct answer.

The incident says that the supervisor was not consulted.

Please go to page X-1

Page X-4

You selected 2: Because they decided they weren't better than the whites after all.

This is not the most correct answer.

The incident does not indicate that the blacks felt superior to the whites. The whites only thought this was so.

Please go to page X-1

Page X-5

You selected 3: Because they realized that it was part of the job.

Yes, this is the best choice.

The black men were probably aware that often in the past blacks had been expected to do the worst jobs. They were unwilling to continue to do the worst jobs. However, when the white man pointed out that it was an unpleasant job that everyone had to do, including the whites, they were willing to cooperate. This problem could have been avoided if this had been pointed out to the blacks when they were first hired and trained.

Please go to page X-7

Page X-6

You selected 4: They knew that Russell had seniority and could tell them what to do.

While Russell did have seniority, he wasn't a supervisor and couldn't order the blacks to work.

Please go to page X-1

METHODS OF DATA COLLECTION

There are several steps that must be gone through in constructing a culture assimilator. These are dealt with below.

The first step is to understand the subjective culture of the members of the trainee's culture and the culture he is trying to understand. For convenience we will call these the "own culture" and the "target culture." Studies of subjective culture, such as the ones discussed in Triandis et al., *The Analysis of Subjective Culture* (1972), and in this book, permit comparisons of the own culture with the target culture. Those features of the two cultures that produce the maximum contrast should be represented in the training. For example, suppose that in the own culture people are expected to show respect in a certain role, but in the target culture this is not the case. We might construct an incident in which a person showed respect when he was not expected to, and the other from the target culture was greatly surprised. More interesting, of course, is the case when the own culture does not show respect and the target culture does. An incident is used as an illustration of each type of situation.

In order to obtain material that could be used in the culture assimilator, we studied the stereotypes that blacks and whites have about significant people in their environment, their behavioral intentions toward such people, their role perceptions, job perceptions, and finally their perceptions of the antecedents and consequents of events.

These particular foci were selected on the basis of two considerations. In previous work, reported in *The Analysis of Subjective Culture,* we (a) developed procedures for the measurement of these domains and (b) learned something about the utility of different kinds of information in constructing culture assimilators. Since an almost infinite number of probes into the subjective culture of a sample are possible, it is important to select those probes which will be likely to provide the most useful material. Similarly, selecting a focus on which we had done work previously meant that we could skip some of the work in developing the instruments for the measurement of the variables of that domain.

In the present chapter we will briefly mention the background of some of the constructs we selected for measurement and will provide references to previous work, so that the interested reader can examine the antecedents of this study.

STEREOTYPES

Humans tend to "type" groups of people, that is, to assume that groups have particular characteristics. For example, many think that Jews are shrewd. What people believe about another group of people defines their stereotype.

Some of these beliefs are relatively accurate. For example, when a person assigns the characteristic "Democrats" to northern blacks, he makes a relatively correct judgment. At least after 1936, the majority of northern blacks (ranging from 64 to 97%) have voted Democratic (Campbell, 1968). On the other hand, there is no objective evidence on the distribution of the characteristic *shrewd*. A point-by-point check of the stereotype of Armenians held in a California community (LaPiere, 1936) revealed that none of the characteristics which people assigned to Armenians were distributed more strongly among Armenians than among other groups.

The best statement that can be made is that some of the beliefs forming a stereotype are accurate, but most are not. The accurate beliefs concern visible traits, that is, traits that have an obvious behavioral outcome. For example, the characteristic *pious* has been found to be assigned relatively accurately to certain tribesmen in East Pakistan (Schuman, 1966) because the trait is manifested in certain behaviors that can be observed daily. Other traits were incorrectly assigned to the same tribesmen. When we have direct experience with a particular category of people, the stereotype is likely to have more accurate elements than when we do not. Otherwise the stereotype reflects mostly the biases of journalists, teachers, and others who have told us what the world is like.

Even though stereotypes may have a "kernel of truth," they are poor ways of making judgments about groups of people, as Campbell (1967) has so well analyzed. This is because, first, there is a sense of absolutism in the stereotype — that is, if a group is said to have a characteristic, *all* members of the group are assumed to have it. This leads to various errors in thinking. For instance, if a group consistently voted for the Democratic party, and we assign the label Democratic to them, in a particular election the vote might be 65% to 35%. The label is accurate for the group as a whole, but what about the 35% who do not fit the label? This is obviously a stereotype that causes errors in judgment.

Second, stereotyping makes people think that there are great similarities among those who are members of a group and great differences between that group and other groups. Most evidence indicates that most human traits are distributed so that there is much overlap among groups. Third, there is a tendency to assume that group membership is the cause of the trait. For example, a person might think: "He voted Democratic *because* he is a northern Negro." In fact, the cause is usually different, and might have to do with the actions of members of the parties that have seemed more equitable to a particular group than to other groups. Hence, again, stereotyping leads to errors in judgment. Fourth, we tend to assign negative stereotypes to groups with whom we are in conflict and positive stereotypes to our friends (Avigdor, 1953). This means, again, that we err when we stereotype any group we strongly like or strongly dislike.

While it would be desirable for humans to stop stereotyping, this is quite impossible because of the complexity of the social environment. We cannot deal with every person as a unique individual, although ideally we should do so. There is just too much information reaching us.

Even when we think of people that we know quite well, we tend to think that they have stable characteristics. For example, we think of our spouses, parents, etc. as having particular characteristics. Furthermore, we carry with us implicit personality theories, that is, ideas about what traits go together. For example, *warm* people are *friendly, fat* people are *jolly,* or *tall* men are *handsome.* While, again, there may be a grain of truth in these generalizations, the use of such beliefs leads to errors in judgment. There is evidence that when a person explains his behavior to himself, he finds the causes in the environment, but when the same behavior is seen by others, they find the causes of it in personality characteristics or other internal attributes (Jones and Nisbett, 1972). In short, there is something inaccurate about the use of personality characteristics even when we know a great deal about another person. Nevertheless, since a person's total behavior involves millions of acts, it is convenient to think of patterns of behavior as being typical of him, and hence to use categories which are *like* stereotypes in thinking about him.

Stereotypes are important because when we judge the actions of another person, we always do it in the context of such stereotypes. For instance, if we know of a *kind* mother, and we see her spanking her child, we are likely to assume that she is "correcting" him. A *cold* mother doing the same might be assumed to be "taking out her frustrations" on him.

BEHAVIORAL INTENTIONS

A good deal of human behavior depends on the intentions that people have concerning their behavior. These intentions are strongly influenced by norms and roles. In addition, the way we feel about the behavior and the perceived consequences of the behavior influences our intentions.

Behavioral intentions are conceived to be the antecedents of behavior. However, behavior is also determined by previous habits, which make much behavior "automatic" (unconscious). Furthermore, situational factors may make a behavior more or less difficult, thus either minimizing or maximizing its probability. In spite of these qualifications, however, behavioral intentions are an important antecedent of behavior. For a review of relevant studies, see Triandis (1975a).

The methodology of measurement of behavioral intentions is available. Triandis (1964) and several others (e.g., Fishbein and Ajzen, 1972, 1973) have used adaptations of the semantic differential for this purpose.

ROLE PERCEPTIONS

It is commonplace to state that people live in groups. Groups develop specializations of functions, so that people who are unusually good at particular jobs do those jobs and others do other jobs. A position within any group often requires certain behaviors. The pattern of behavior associated with a position is a "role." By extension, we find roles in societies. Thus any patterned sequence of learned behaviors performed by a person in an interaction situation might be considered a role (Sarbin, 1954). This pattern of behavior is normative in the sense that it is particularly appropriate for persons holding positions in a social system.

Linton (1936) was one of the first to use the role concept in theoretical analyses of group behavior. It refers to the dynamic, action component of the status of an individual in a social system. The theoretical discussion of roles has produced a rich literature (e.g., Biddle and Thomas, 1966; Sarbin and Allen, 1968). There was less done on the empirical level, although both Sarbin (1954) and Sarbin and Allen (1968) have reviewed a number of empirical procedures. The most extensive studies of role perception were done by Triandis (Triandis, Vassiliou, and Nassiakou, 1968; Triandis, McGuire, Saral, Yang, Loh, and Vassiliou, 1972). Such investigations have revealed the presence of some basic dimensions of role perception: (a) giving or denying love (affect), (b) giving or denying status, and (c) intimacy versus formality. These dimensions appear in different mixtures all around the world in studies of role perception.

JOB PERCEPTIONS

An important aspect of any social environment consists of jobs. Young people today are asking "What jobs are available?" "How good are they?" "What does one have to do to get this job?" "What will one obtain from such a job?" These are important questions. Variations in job perceptions do exist, and tell us something about the way different samples of people look at jobs.

Earlier studies of job perception, such as Triandis (1960), have suggested some of the dimensions which people use in thinking about jobs. In that study five dimensions were important: (a) objective job evaluation (requires experience, good, important, professional, creative, requires much education and training); (b) white collar (indoors, soft, clean, office work, light, sitting); (c) variable (changeable, new, executive, creative); (d) level (high position, steady, high pay, difficult, doing many things); and (e) subjective job evaluation (desirable, good, important, responsible, alert, active, ingenious, creative, interesting, challenging).

In the present study we utilized attributes of jobs that our samples gave to us spontaneously but also added, as marker variables, one attribute that represented each of these five dimensions.

IMPLICATIVE RELATIONSHIPS

A major characteristic of human thought is that concepts appear connected to other concepts. While nineteenth-century associationism led to several important psychological studies, a more focused approach which examines the perceived antecedents (what causes or precedes an event) and consequents (what follows an event) of events seems easier to work with. This is particularly true in cross-cultural studies where the heterogeneity and richness of the data reach a maximum.

In *The Analysis of Subjective Culture* Triandis et al. (1972) examined the perceived antecedents and consequents of 20 value concepts among samples of Americans, Greeks, Indians, and Japanese. The procedure consisted of asking the respondents to finish sentences of the form "If you have . . ., then you have Peace," or "If you have Peace, then you have. . . ." The first sentence-type yields the antecedents and the second the consequents of Peace. Lists of antecedents and consequents of each of the 20 concepts were obtained in each culture. These lists were combined so that one-fifth of the antecedents or consequents were "culture-common," one-fifth were given in the pretests only by the American sample, one-fifth by the Greek, one-fifth by the Indian, and one-fifth by the Japanese sample. Numerous differences in emphasis, favoring particular antecedents and consequents of concepts, were found in that investigation. These differences suggested that the method yields data consistent with ethnographic observations of cultural differences.

In the present study we examined the antecedents and consequents of concepts that we considered important in analyzing the thought patterns of blacks and whites. In selecting incidents to illustrate the differences in subjective culture, we might also consider the guidelines that are implied by our earlier analysis — namely, that the more abstract the elements of subjective culture, the more important they are in understanding the difficulties that will be generated by behavior which is inconsistent with the other person's expectations.

A very different method for developing incidents is to employ Flanagan's (1954) method of "critical incidents." Here people from both the own and the target culture are asked to think of any incident in which something happened that changed their mind, either positively or negatively, about members of the other culture. This can be done by interviewing. In one study we tried telephone interviews in order to get a broader sample of informants, but people seemed too inhibited on the phone and we obtained very few incidents. Face-to-face interviews are necessary.

Item Construction

The incidents obtained from the critical-incident method can be edited to be most sharply relevant to the differences in subjective culture which we wish to teach. In addition, incidents can be written just the way a playwright writes a play. The author uses his imagination. The incidents are constructed so that they make the points we wish to make. The four attributions that correspond to each incident can best be obtained by presenting the incident to members of cultures A and B (own and target) and asking them to make attributions. Then, by selecting the types of attributions that are made by members of culture A but not B, and members of B but not A, we have four attributions, three likely to be given by members of culture A and one likely to be given in culture B. When training members of culture A to understand the viewpoint of members of culture B, the answers given by members of culture B are considered correct and those given by members of culture A incorrect.

Editing the Items

The complete incident and four attributions at this stage are presented to members of cultures A and B who are asked to "criticize" the items from the point of view of whether they are believable or offensive, and to judge which of the four attributions is correct. This sample of subjects gives information which is used in rewriting and editing the items so they do indeed guide the trainee in the direction of learning about the other culture without offending him or members of the target culture. The latter requirement is often difficult to meet, since members of some target cultures appear to be exceptionally sensitive. We have often had to settle for incidents which are only "mildly offensive" rather than completely inoffensive.

Validity Studies

Once several hundred incidents are assembled into several volumes, we can do two kinds of studies: (a) studies in which trained and untrained individuals work with members of another culture in experimental settings, and (b) field studies in which we follow trained and untrained individuals over a period of time and record objective indices of good interpersonal relationships (invitations, testimonials, marriages, etc.) and bad relationships (fights, divorces, etc.).

More specifically, in industrial settings we planned to observe the job satisfaction and turnover and absenteeism rates of workers who work for trained and untrained foremen. Since our practical purpose was to increase the probability of blacks staying in white industrial environments, we developed culture assimilators for both whites and blacks. This can lead to a design in which trained or untrained foremen and trained or untrained workers are observed over a one-year period. The design calls for four groups (all combinations mentioned above).

One point about the assimilator should be made clear. Like any other book, it provides information. People who are not motivated to learn this information will not do so. In short, if the environment of the foreman does not motivate him to do well in his relations with minority group members, the assimilator will not help. It is extremely important to consider the equation: success equals motivation times knowledge. The assimilator provides the knowledge. The setting, including how people get rewarded, by whom and for what, is an essential element for the success of a program. On the other hand, motivation alone will also not lead to success. No matter how much motivation and good will there might be, the foremen will make mistakes leading to vicious circles of poor interpersonal relationships unless they know how to avoid these mistakes. Such knowhow requires studying the culture assimilator.

Comparison with Other Methods of Culture Training

Many procedures are available for cross-cultural training. Wight (1969) summarized these procedures, including the culture assimilator, in his handbook. Here we will briefly mention the most important methods.

To begin with, one can read a book about the other culture. The problem is that a book may have more information than the trainee cares to have, or the information may not be particularly relevant for behavior in the other culture. Furthermore, the information is often too abstract, so that the reader does not know how to apply it to his situation.

One can send the person to the culture he is supposed to learn about, and let him find out first-hand. The problem here is that this takes much time, and in some cases it can literally be dangerous.

One can role-play being a member of another culture. This is fine if one knows about the other culture, so that he *can* role-play. But most people do not know enough about the other culture to do a good job of role-playing.

One can read case studies of behavior in the other culture. This is already very similar to what is done in the assimilator.

One can arrange encounter groups, T-groups, etc. in which members from both cultures are present. This is fine, as long as we combine this experience with information about the other culture. Without such information the experience is often more frustrating than enlightening. For example, a T-group session involving foreign students discussing their "problems" with American students, which Triandis observed at Cornell University in 1969, proved most frustrating and disintegrated in anger.

Behavior modification techniques can be used. Here a person identifies what is reinforcing to persons from other cultures and he agrees to emit more reinforcements to such persons. However, such techniques also require cultural training and understanding of the subjective culture of the people in question. The assimilator can be added to this experience.

In short, the assimilator is a relatively brief experience that adds a strong component of cultural information. It can be used singly or in combination with other techniques.

Any cross-cultural training technique should be rigorously evaluated. Unfortunately, there are very few evaluation studies of the cultural training methods mentioned above. The only exception is the culture assimilator, which has been evaluated (Fiedler, Mitchell, and Triandis, 1971) with promising results (Brislin, 1970).

CHAPTER THREE

Black and White Subjective Culture: An Introduction

H. C. TRIANDIS, J. FELDMAN,

D. E. WELDON, AND W. HARVEY

The literature on black Americans is so extensive that a review can only list some of the better volumes and comment on the very best. Starting with Myrdal's (1944) classic work, available in paperback (Rose, 1948), through Pettigrew's (1964) *Profile of the Negro American,* to Miller and Dreger's (1973) tome, which summarizes a voluminous literature on some 25 different topics, there is a rich literature on every aspect of black behavior. The National Institute of Mental Health (1972) published a *Bibliography on Racism,* while Ehrlich (1973) provided a recent systematic social psychological treatment. Broad collections of psychological papers (Baughman, 1971; Goldschmid, 1970; Jones, 1972; Wilcox, 1971) provide perspectives from both black and white psychologists. More specialized treatments focus on topics such as identity formation (Hauser, 1971) or employment.

Problems of employment have received so much attention that there is a 60-page annotated bibliography (Pinto and Buchmeier, 1973) just on that topic. Among the more notable books on the topic, one should mention Purcell and Cavanagh (1972), Ruthledge and Gass (1967), Ross and Wheeler (1971), and Ferman (1968).

The anthropological perspectives must include a range of books, starting with those written by blacks to explain the black experience, among the best of which is *The Autobiography of Malcolm X* (Haley and Malcolm X, 1964) and Deutscher and Thompson (1968). Less useful, though important, are black protests such as Fanon (1967) and Lester (1968). Among the best ethnographies are Hannerz (1969) and Suttles (1968).

If forced to choose one book among the rich fare that is available, we would select Valentine (1968). Valentine criticizes the pejorative tradition established by Frazier (1932, 1966) and expanded by Glazer and Moynihan (1963), which reflects middle-class perspectives such as those of Walter Miller (1958). He also raises many questions concerning the notion that there is a "culture of poverty," as argued by Lewis (1959, 1960, 1961, 1966). He challenges these views with ammunition from Clark (1965), Gladwin (1967), Keil (1966), and Liebow (1967). His critique is sometimes devastating, sometimes overstated, but consistently scholarly. It provides the best introduction to the topic and the most defensible point of view. It summarizes the major viewpoints with admirable clarity. These viewpoints do not represent the position of any one writer but, rather, "schools" of thought on the subject. For the present summary of the literature, they provide the most succinct presentation.

The first major viewpoint is that there is a culture of poverty; it is a self-perpetuating subculture of the major society with a defective, unhealthy way of life. It is disorganized, pathological, and an incomplete version of middle-class culture. It is self-generating because of socialization practices that perpetuate its psychological inadequacies, blocking escape from poverty. The proposed model of "training" is to assimilate the subculture into the middle class or working class. This can be accomplished through social work, psychiatry, and education.

The second point of view argues that there are oppressed and exploited subcultures. The pathology has its source in the total system. The disadvantaged position of the poor is maintained by the higher social strata, to preserve their advantages. The proposed "training" is to come after a revolution, which must destroy the total structure.

The third point of view, and the one which is defended by Valentine, is that the lower-class poor do indeed possess some distinct subcultural patterns, even though they subscribe to norms similar to those of the mainstream. On some dimensions they overlap with the mainstream while on others they are different. The distinctive patterns include both pathogenic traits and also healthy elements which maximize creative adaptation to conditions of deprivation. Both socialization patterns and exploitation cause the behavioral patterns that are observed. Training requires three kinds of changes: modifications in the institutions of the total society, modifications in the institutions of the poor, and a shift in resources from the larger society to the poor.

The first viewpoint has been the orthodox view of American academics and governments in recent years. Valentine reviews evidence that is inconsistent with it, but does not deny that many of the facts are consistent with aspects of this position. The second viewpoint is the one argued by the radical left. Valentine argues that it is incomplete, but that the evidence is somewhat more consistent with that viewpoint than it is with the first. Exploitation in the form of wage differentials, "black jobs," etc. is a factor which cannot be denied. The third model is eclectic and uses the strong points of both previous models. Valentine outlines an imaginative program of employment of the poor, supported by the federal government, with several components of training.

Several themes emerge from our own study which are broadly consistent with Valentine's analysis. The first is what we will call "eco-system distrust." By eco-system distrust we mean that an individual distrusts every aspect of his environment, including the idea that the parts of the environment influence each other in lawful ways.

Another important point is that both blacks and whites are extraordinarily heterogeneous. There are more similarities in the responses of blacks and whites than there are differences. One important similarity is that both racial groups are quite heterogeneous. There are several black points of view. The evidence on this point comes from the analyses of the way blacks respond to stereotypes and behavioral intentions, as well as the diversity of the responses to the what-leads-to-what questionnaires (implicative relationships). For example, in Phase II of our studies the black high school students very frequently responded the same way as the white college students, while the black hardcore of this phase responded quite differently, often like the white high school students of the same study. The suggestion here is that blacks who go to high school, even when they attend a special program for "problem students," have adopted a point of view that is *relatively* middle class. By contrast, the white high school students with "problems," attending the same high school, share some of their points of view with the hardcore unemployed blacks.

The hardcore blacks, however, stand out more often than not. They seem to be different from other groups in many ways. Moreover, we should speak of two kinds of them: "problem hardcore," as studied in Phase II, and "ordinary hardcore," as found in Phase III. The problem hardcore seem to be demoralized. For example, they see most people as unimportant and untrustworthy, and they do not consider it appropriate to help and respect members of their own family. By way of contrast, there is a militant group of blacks who favor revolution and have a very positive view of black men. This latter group responds in the same way as whites to questions concerning relationships within the family. The problem hardcore entered the sample because they asked for help in coping with their problems. The ordinary hardcore sample was approached by a survey research organization because they met the established criteria for membership in this category.

Other themes emerging in the data are that interracial conflict is symmetric. The commonsense expectation of suspicion across racial lines is well supported by the data. There is a tendency for blacks to be more hostile toward white men than the other way around; however, white women do not receive the same degree of black rejection.

The one fact that is most striking here is the great similarity in the rejection of each race for the other. Furthermore, there are no racial differences in responses to events reflecting political conflict. It is as though conflict has a transparent quality which involves agreement to disagree and to reject.

The black hardcore had conceptions of work roles that were different from those found in other samples. Specifically, there was a tendency for the blacks to expect more formal, more subordinate, and more friendly relationships on the job than was the case with the whites. Second, the hardcore blacks often had an "irresponsible" viewpoint concerning jobs (e.g., they saw looking for fun leading to skipping work and this not leading to guilt). They also had a cynical view of work situations (e.g., if you get a raise, you get little additional satisfaction, so you do not increase your efforts on the job). This was not the case with the white middle class.

This very sketchy summary gives some of the flavor of the findings that will be detailed in the following chapters. The next chapter is a report on differences in the meaning of words in the black and white communities. This chapter includes the method, results, and discussion of the findings about the meaning of words. Next, there is a chapter which reports the methodology used to arrive at the findings reported in Chapters 6 and 7.

CHAPTER FOUR

Word Meanings in Black and White

D. LANDIS, P. MC GREW, H. DAY,
J. SAVAGE, AND T. SARAL

INTRODUCTION AND BACKGROUND

The following incident happened in the secretarial section of a company: Sally, a young white female, was attempting to make a special impression on her supervisor one day. She put on her best clothes and made sure her appearance was especially nice. When she arrived at work, Martha, her black co-worker, smiled at her and said, "Girl, you look *bad*." Sally was hurt, for she assumed that Martha was being critical. The fact that Martha was really being quite complimentary is irrelevant to Sally's feelings, since Sally lacked the cognitive structure to correctly decode Martha's statement.

Blacks' use of language has undoubtedly produced misunderstandings similar to the one described above. That is, it is likely that black patois terminology used among some blacks (also known as "Black English") is not always understood by others. It would be beyond the scope of this chapter to examine the historical roots of the various black patois. Whatever their origins, it is clear that the meanings of the words used are sufficiently at variance from their use in standard American English to provide the potential for serious misunderstandings between some blacks and whites.

For many years the serious study of Black English (BE) has been

The research reported here was supported by the following grants: Educational Testing Service Grant No. 865-12 to D. Landis (pilot work); National Science Foundation and National Institute of Mental Health grants to C. E. Osgood (data analysis); National Science Foundation Grant No. GS 30952X to D. Landis (data gathering and report preparation as well as supplementary data analyses). The opinions in this chapter are those of the authors and do not necessarily represent embroiled in controversy. While most early scholars tended to consider BE to be a dialect (largely southern in origin) of standard English (AE) with little integrity of its own, others took a more pernicious point of view. Differences in syntax, for example, between BE and AE, were considered to be produced by faulty learning of the rules of AE construction. Such errors could not, then, be consistent and representative of a well-worked-out language structure. Apropos of this point, Hall and Freedle (1973) have provided data which suggest that BE is, in form, similar to all other languages; it is in the specific content that differences with AE appear. This study is supportive of the linguistic analysis of Labov and Robins (1965). These are particularly important studies in that other researchers have used the apparent characteristics of BE to suggest that blacks and low socioeconomic-status (SES) populations in general are not able to utilize the language to express abstract concepts (e.g., Hess and Shipman, 1965). The implications of such studies are obvious, since the ability to deal in abstractions is linked to economic advancement through success in educational institutions. However, as Baratz and Baratz (1970) and Hall and Landis (in preparation) point out, these studies have such serious methodological flaws as to make their results highly questionable.

The studies of Labov and his colleagues, while interesting, deal with only one aspect of language — its rules of construction, or syntax. As Morris noted in 1939, one can discuss language from three points of view: its rules of construction (syntax), the rules which relate words to objects (semantics), and the rules covering usage (pragmatics). It is in the second domain of "semiotics" (Pierce, 1955) — semantics — that we come to an area of inquiry that has bedeviled psychologists for at least a century. We are referring to the problem of meaning. Allport (1955) expressed it well when he noted that "meaning, a concept born under the malediction of introspection, bandied about by

positions of the various grantors. The first author wishes to indicate that order of authorship of this report does not imply anything about the level of effort in either conducting the research or preparing this chapter.

We wish to express our appreciation to C. E. Osgood and W. H. May of the University of Illinois, who not only performed the data analyses for this research but also graciously provided the "white" data which are reported. Their support, both financially and affectively, is gratefully acknowledged here. Prof. Osgood's thoughtful critique of an earlier version is much appreciated, but responsibility for interpretation rests with the authors.

philosophers, overformalized by configurationists, disguised by behaviorists who could not afford to disown it, has been a stepchild in psychology" (p. 574).

Thus the problem of meaning (or as Ogden and Richards, 1949, put it, *The Meaning of Meaning*) has, like its theoretical brother, consciousness, caused philosophical and psychological questions complicated enough to "cross a rabbi's eyes." If philosophers and linguists have been argumentative, is it any wonder that psychologists have not been less confused?

It is not the purpose of this chapter to enter into a detailed discussion of the psychological theories of meaning or even of the extensive corpus of relevant empirical studies. That has been done elsewhere (e.g., Osgood, Suci, and Tannenbaum, 1957; Osgood, 1971; Creelman, 1966). However, we should indicate that one such approach, neobehaviorism, has led directly to the measurement technique that is used in this chapter (Osgood, 1971).

Briefly, such an approach holds that the meaning of a concept is defined as the sum total of the internal responses which have been previously reinforced when that concept is elicited. These responses have both antagonistic and intensity properties, the first property giving rise to the idea of bi-polarity and the second, the concept of continuity. Thus in order to measure these responses, a behavioral technique is necessary which also manifests the above properties. From this theoretical consideration (Osgood, Suci, and Tannenbaum, 1957; Osgood, 1971) it was a short step to the development of the semantic differential (Osgood and Suci, 1955; Osgood, Suci, and Tannenbaum, 1957).

Osgood (1971, p. 9, italics added) describes the semantic differential as follows:

When in semantic differential (SD) technique a sample of subjects rates a sample of concepts against a sample of *7-step* scales defined by *verbal opposites,* a cube of data is generated — the rows representing scales, the columns concepts, and the slices from front to back individual subjects. Each cell in the cube contains a value from $+3$ to -3 and represents a particular subject's judgment of a particular item, e.g.:

TORNADO

fair____:____:____:____:____:____:__X__unfair

The italicized portions of the above quotation should serve to show the relation of SD to the underlying behavioral model. Once the data cube is generated, it is necessary to simplify and interpret the results. Since the number of possible bi-polar adjectives that one can use is very large (the "original" SD consists of 50 bi-polar scales), and since it is likely that many of the scales will be correlated with other scales, some technique of data reduction is desirable. Usually factor analysis is used.

Because factor analysis appears to be quite complex for the uninitiated, a full discussion of the technique is quite beyond the scope of this chapter. However, with regard to SD data, factor analysis accomplishes

... a representation of all the variance of usage (e.g., of 50 scales) in terms of the underlying set of dimensions or factors ordered in terms of the proportions of variance they account for. Thus, if all of the 50 "lines" defined by verbal opposites could be represented in a solid three-dimensional space without distorting their mathematical relationships — thus truly a cushion with 50 intersecting pins — then only three underlying factors would necessarily be sufficient since the correlations between all pairs of scales could be accounted for exactly by *their* projections onto the three underlying factors. [Osgood, 1971, p. 11]

Osgood's use of the example of three factors is not exactly accidental, for "SD technique typically yields three dominant affective factors ... : Evaluation (Good/Bad), Potency (Strong/Weak), and Activity (Active/Passive)" (Osgood, 1971, p. 14).

In fact, the conclusion about Evaluation, Potency, and Activity (EPA) can be expressed more strongly than it is above: "... *given diversified samples of concepts, scales, and native informants, the EPA structure of the semantic space obtained in replications of the SD technique is non-arbitrary*. Just as there is non-arbitrariness of the geophysical space, determined by gravity, the rotation of our planet, and the location of the magnetic pole, so there seemed to be non-arbitrariness in the affective meaning space" (Osgood, 1971, p. 19, italics in the original).

Indeed, the first report of the semantic differential in the middle 1950s stimulated such an outpouring of research reporting similar conclusions that, by comparison, the above statement seems almost modest. One compendium of papers dealing with the semantic differential indicated that in the period between 1955 and 1969, over 1,500 articles used the technique (Bobren, Hill, Snider, and Osgood, 1969). Few other techniques have enjoyed such wide acceptance. And the commonality of results is such that we can agree with Heise (1969) that the SD has become the standard technique for studying affective meaning including attitudes.[1]

It has been necessary to give the reader the preceding brief background on the SD to place in perspective our cross-cultural study, especially since it involves black American populations, which are the central concern in this chapter.[2] In response to the question of where the current studies fit into the SD research literature, we ask the following questions: (1) Is the meaning structure of black Americans adequately and parsimoniously represented by EPA? (2) If so, are the meanings of specific concepts (as represented by EPA factor loadings) the same in black American populations compared to white American groups?

These questions become important when we note that most of the original SD data came from studies on native white American populations. Put another way, the "... research ... had been highly ethnocentric — focused on humans sharing a common (American) culture and speaking a common (English) language ..." (Osgood, 1971, p. 19). Thus it is reasonable to ask about the generality of the EPA semantic meaning system. Beginning in 1956, Osgood and his colleagues (Triandis and Osgood, 1958) set out to gather data bearing on the pervasiveness of EPA in different cultural and language systems.

In attempting cross-cultural research, there are certain conceptual and practical problems that must be addressed. However, there are excellent sources available on these problems and their solutions (e.g., Osgood, 1971; Werner and Campbell, 1970; Triandis, et al., *The Analysis of Subjective Culture,* 1972). Therefore, we shall not engage in an extensive discussion here, except to point out that the use of the

---

[1] The basis for the use of the SD in the study of attitudes stems from the finding that the E factor correlates highly with Thurstone and Guttman attitude scales. Osgood and his associates concluded: "The findings ... support the notion that evaluative factor is an index of attitudes" (Osgood, Suci, and Tannenbaum pp. 194-195).

[2] This is a good point at which to remind the reader that the use of "black" and "white" refer to *particular samples of black and white* This is a convenient shorthand rather than an all-inclusive generalizati' we do feel that there probably would be substantial generalization ac white samples beyond the specific groups we report, this supposit' verified by further research.

SD in cross-cultural research was marked by a scrupulous fidelity to the concept of obtaining indigenous structures. Indeed, with all the care that was applied, it is impressive that EPA regularly and clearly appeared in the nearly 30 cultures studied to date (Osgood, 1971). The procedures used in these studies will be described in more detail in a later section of this chapter, where they may be discussed in the context of word usage among certain segments of the black American population.

When the SD research enterprise moved beyond American shores (to over 25 wide-ranging areas of the world), an unfortunate result occurred. Most American researchers seemed to forget that the United States itself is a very heterogeneous culture. There tended to be an implicit assumption that the original AE data could be applied willy-nilly to various American subgroups, including black Americans. From about 1965 there was fairly widespread use of the semantic differential in such studies. These studies were undoubtedly stimulated by the entry of the federal government into programs for the disadvantaged and the consequent need for easily administered evaluation instruments (Landis, Hayman, and Hall, 1971). In particular, many of these programs stated as one of their goals the "improvement of self-image" among the target populations. Given what we know about the properties of the semantic differential, it would appear to be an ideally useful instrument. Given also what we know about word usage among certain blacks and their culture, it is not surprising that these studies (even those that were well designed) gave conflicting and often confusing results. Of the studies that have appeared in the years following 1957 related to the semantic differential, relatively few have involved members of American ethnic/racial groups.[3] Numerous studies have used groups of subjects in which race is unspecified (e.g., Heaps, 1972; Komorita and Bass, 1967), but it is highly probable, judging by inspection of the limited subject descriptions, that some percentage of

[3] One notable exception is a study of semantic structures in American Southwest culture groups by Suci (1960), in which comparisons were made between American Indian and Spanish-speaking bilinguals using the stringent methods of construction of indigenous semantic differentials employed by Osgood and his associates. The results, with the exception of the Navajo group, showed a high degree of similarity in factor structure to all other culture groups studied. However, these results should be viewed with some caution, since the subjects were all bilingual, unlike the studies in other cultures which were based on data from monolingual subjects.

the subjects were members of American minorities. From our search of the literature it appears that possible racial differences in semantic structure have yet to be investigated. This is somewhat surprising in view of the increasing body of literature on significant linguistic differences between speakers of Black English and standard American English (cf. Hooper and Powell, 1971; Hall and Freedle, 1973; Stewart, 1969; Baratz, 1969). And in the majority of studies which *have* specified the racial makeup of the subjects, the investigators in every case used for both blacks and whites the American English semantic differential which employs 12 of the original 50 standard bi-polar adjective scales with the highest loadings on the E, P, and A factors.

White and Richmond (1970) examined the perception of self and peers in economically deprived black and advantaged white fifth graders in Georgia by administering Coopersmith's Self-esteem Inventory and Osgood's 12-scale American English semantic differential. Because of the paper's brevity, it is difficult to understand exactly to what treatments the data were subjected. It is more difficult to follow the authors' interpretations of the results, which led to the following conclusions: "Apparently, a great deal of congruence was evident between self-concepts and peer perceptions in both groups of fifth graders. The largest contributor to the perceptions of these advantaged white and disadvantaged black children toward the sociometry of their classrooms was the feeling about 'activity' (SD) in their peers." Finally, ". . . there was a high similarity in the way they perceived themselves and their classmates." No further explanations or elaborations are given, and little light is shed on the authors' stated attempt to investigate the correlations between black self-feelings and academic achievement compared to whites. It may be of some significance that the data from almost 25% of the black children in the sample were eliminated because of "reading disability."

A study conducted a year later at the same university (University of Georgia; Hooper and Powell, 1971) investigated language comprehension in 129 rural (75% black) children in Georgia. These subjects were tested in standard English, "dialect," and a mixture of both. The children ". . . had difficulty performing even simple language tasks when the task was confounded by mixtures of dialect and teacher SE (standard English)." The difficulties encountered were in ". . . translating from standard English to dialect, and vice versa. . . ." It would be valuable and interesting to see what relationships might be found between self-feelings and academic achievement among black and white children if each group were tested in the language, dialect, or style most comprehensible to them.

Several studies employed the semantic differential with black as well as white subjects to investigate responses to color names as indices of racial attitudes (Williams, 1964; Farber and Schmeidler, 1971; Williams, Tucker, and Dunham, 1971). John Williams (1964) found significant differences in the connotative meanings of five "race-related" (black, white, red, yellow, brown) and five control (blue, green, purple, orange, gray) color names. Williams hypothesized that "1) the color names white and black would differ systematically in connotative meaning along the evaluative (good/bad) dimension with white viewed more positively than black; and 2) the difference between the evaluative connotations . . . would not be as great for Negroes *S*s as for Caucasians *S*s." Using the 12-scale American English semantic differential, he found, in brief, that white was viewed similarly by both blacks and whites as good, weak, and active, and black was bad (Caucasian) to neutral (Negro), strong, and passive, confirming both hypotheses. The author discusses possible relationships to the connotative meanings of color names traditionally assigned to ethnic and racial groups to the development of attitudes toward those groups.

In 1971 Williams, Tucker, and Dunham investigated whether significant changes had occurred in color-name connotation among groups of blacks and whites since Williams's 1964 study described above. Citing the growth of the "black identity" movement in the middle and late 1960s, the purpose of the study was to determine if parallel changes had occurred in the connotative meanings of black and white. Additionally, the investigators devised and employed a black separatism scale to assess the effect of "the degree of ideological commitment to black separatism among the Negro subjects. . . ." The scale involved asking black subjects to which of six national civil rights organizations they would like to belong. The six organizations were ranked by a group of black students and faculty (showing 100% agreement) from *most* to *least* separatist, and a separatist score was determined from black subjects' choices. The 12-scale American English semantic differential identical to that used in the 1964 study was administered to all subjects, again using five race-related and five control color names. For the black subjects the results showed significant changes: "... black became more positive (good) and more active, with its connotations of strength remaining unchanged; white became less positive and less active, with no change in its connotations of weakness." There were no significant changes for whites in connotative meanings of any of the ten color names. The authors concluded that because no significant differences were found for blacks in either the other three race-related colors (yellow, red, and brown) or the non-race-related colors between the 1964 and 1971 studies, the effect of the black identity movement on the color names black and white was selective and restricted to the black subculture. The results for black subjects "most strongly committed to the black separatist movement" were the most dramatic but did *not*, alone, account for the significant changes found for blacks between the 1964 and 1971 studies.

In the same year Farber and Schmeidler (1971) tested differences in black and white seventh graders' responses to the color names black and white and compared their findings to John Williams's 1964 study. The three classes tested differed in reading ability: poor, average, and good. The data from the class identified as good readers were excluded because it included no black children. The authors modified the 12-scale American English semantic differential in several ways. They reduced the seven points of the scales to five, a common procedure in administering the semantic differential to children. But they also changed several of the adjective pairs "to simplify the original." The authors gave no rationale for the selection of the simpler adjectives. Although by inspection the changes appear reasonable (*sacred-profane* became *holy-unholy*, for example), this affects the comparability of the data with those of Williams, who used the 12 scales demonstrated to have the highest loadings on the EPA factors. The results for whites confirmed Williams's (1964) findings: black was evaluated significantly less favorably and more potently than white, and "... activity showed a non-significant trend in the same direction as Williams' " (Farber and Schmeidler, 1971). For blacks, black was significantly more potent than white, but Evaluation and Activity "... showed non-significant trends in the direction opposite to Williams' data" (Farber and Schmeidler, 1971). These results were closer to those from Williams's later study (Williams, Tucker, and Dunham, 1971),

a fact anticipated by the present authors' observation that the "...
differences between Williams' (1964) data on Negroes and these suggest marked regional differences or *marked change with time,* or
(of course) both. The implication is that Negroes are becoming...
more favorable to black ..." (Farber and Schmeidler, 1971, italics
added). Another finding was that white children with better reading
ability rated black less favorably than poor readers, which the authors
considered an artifact of the semantic differential reflecting the poor
readers' difficulty with words.

Two studies by Warren Williams (1971, 1972) should be mentioned. The earlier study dealt with possible differences between high
and low SES children in perception of concepts formed of personality
test items, using the 12-scale American English semantic differential.
The author noted that the SES differences he did in fact find were
dependent upon the important assumption that "... members of different SES classes did not respond differently to the SD technique itself
and that measured differences reflected different perceptions of the
meaning of the concept, not different reactions to the testing instrument" (Williams, 1971). The second study (1972) investigated this
assumption and used each adjective of the 12 scale pairs as a concept
(resulting in 24 concepts) with low and middle SES subjects. Significant differences were found between the SES groups "... in the ratings
on the most salient factor, the evaluative dimension" (Williams, 1972).

In these studies fifth-grade children differentiated by socioeconomic
status served as subjects. Low SES children in each study were identified only as coming from an inner-city school in a large city and by
sex. Given the proximity of Williams's university (Eastern Michigan)
to the city of Detroit, and the high probability that *some* portion of
the low SES inner-city school sample is black, whether racial differences in the responses to the 12-scale American English semantic differential confounded the results is unfortunately unknown. Since each
of the two studies deals directly or indirectly with differential responses
to the semantic differential itself, one seemingly necessary control
would be to keep race constant. Lacking this information, one must
view the results attributed to the major variable with caution, since
the reported design does not permit the disentangling of SES from
race.

Two papers by McNamara, Ayrer, and Farber (1972) and Ayrer

and Farber (1972) are important in the context of the preceding discussion. Each study reports aspects of a larger study conducted in Philadelphia to develop semantic differential scales for use with inner-city elementary and junior high pupils. The procedure the authors used in the development of the scales adheres closely to that employed by Osgood and his associates in the development of the original American and subsequent cross-cultural semantic differentials. The scales generated in the study differ in a number of ways from those used in the standard semantic differential: some apparently relate to adult relationships, school experience, peer relationships, and physical characteristics of other people. A number of scales included adjectives identical to some of Osgood's, but differing in the adjectives seen as polar opposites. The 861 pupils in the study are identified only by grade level and socioeconomic level. The percentage of black children in the Philadelphia school system, which includes the predominantly white perimeter, is over 60%. The black population in the inner-city area makes up an even greater percentage of the school population. Therefore, there is little doubt that a substantial proportion of the subjects in the study were black children. The lack of precise specificity of the ethnicity of subjects raises the same questions posed of studies mentioned earlier in this review. This is especially unfortunate because the results are interesting and potentially important for future semantic differential research with children.

A common thread running through the attempts to use the semantic differential with black subjects was the failure to consider these individuals as possibly representative of a separate language/culture group (or, at least, in some sense bilingual.) The statement of the problem here does not mean that we accept (or reject) the hypothesis of black cultural uniqueness. But, given the anthropological, historical, and sociological data, such a hypothesis is at least tenable. That being the case, it would seem reasonable to apply the same techniques to scale and concept development that would be used in a geographically separate foreign culture. If EPA results and the semantic ratings of the concepts are the same as those given by white subjects, then and only then would the AE version be justified in practice. It is the purpose of the present chapter to provide data on this question.

In the pages that follow we shall detail the development of a semantic differential in which the concepts and scales are phrased in the black patois used by lower SES urban blacks, specifically those in the West Side of Chicago. We realize that this is an extreme group, not representative of the majority of blacks because of their severe economic deprivation and alienation from the majority culture. It is felt, however, that if EPA results and semantic ratings of the concepts do differ from those given by white subjects, these differences would be reflected among this extreme population. In the future this kind of study will be conducted using blacks of varied SES: it is possible that there may be differences among blacks according to socioeconomic class. Before we plunge deeply into the methodology, we wish to address another question: So what? Suppose we do find a semantic space which is unique to black Americans — of what use is the information?

First of all, let us consider the issue of self-concept of black Americans. Many data have been produced (e.g., Long and Henderson, 1968) presumably demonstrating that black Americans have a low or negative image of themselves. This hypothesis has permeated our educational structure to the point that programs are proposed and funded which are directed to rectifying this situation. If, by using appropriately designed measurements, one could determine that this hypothesis is unwarranted, then the pragmatic implications should be obvious. Not only would such programs be unnecessary, but the funds so allocated could perhaps be spent in more critical areas.

Second, many educational programs (not necessarily directed toward self-image change) require attitude measurement for evaluation purposes. When these programs are directed toward black pupils, an accurate instrument is a necessity. Should the data indicate a different meaning space, with particular reference to educationally meaningful concepts, then a rational basis for program evaluation and modification becomes available. With such a technique at hand, it then becomes possible to make program decisions which involve large expenditures of public funds on the basis of reliable and valid data.

The two considerations discussed above are not trivial. Compensatory education is perhaps one of the most pressing tasks facing American education. It may well be that the pessimistic conclusions of some observers (e.g., Jensen, 1969; Jenck, 1973) are due to inadequate measuring instruments rather than the inability of the children to profit from the programs. If this is so, then faulty programs have continued to receive funding, while possibly effective efforts have been consigned to the project termination file. Any such decision based on data that are methodologically suspect is expensive in both fiscal and human costs.

Also of importance is the contribution that the data can make to a more precise understanding of the psychology of black Americans. To the extent that such knowledge, through the educative process, begins to infiltrate into the white population at large, then the potential for misunderstanding will be decreased. We conceive of this process beginning through the availability of materials in the post-secondary institutions, particularly those that train personnel for our public schools. These personnel will, in turn, teach individuals who will enter occupations (e.g., policemen, social workers, firemen, city workers, etc.) which require daily interaction between black and white. While we cannot expect important changes to occur in the short term, it is this process by which society changes its stereotypes of groups of individuals. This long-term process of change, while more difficult to observe, is nonetheless the more promising in terms of significance and permanence of effects.

To summarize, the objectives of the present study were the following: (1) To develop a semantic differential in which the concepts and scales are phrased in the black patois (BP) of lower SES urban blacks. (2) To compare the scale factor structure of such a semantic differential to that of the AE (mainly white American English) version. (3) To compare the semantic profiles of the concepts obtained from a black sample to those obtained from a white sample. In developing the methods to achieve these goals, we attempted to avoid the problems and pitfalls which have rendered prior research on black Americans methodologically suspect.

METHOD AND PROCEDURE

SCALE DEVELOPMENT

In order to identify a set of adjectives which are frequently used by lower SES urban black subjects, the following procedures were adopted.

1. Translation procedure. One hundred nouns used by Osgood and his collaborators in their cross-cultural studies were translated by ten individuals. The translators, whose ages ranged from late adolescence to early twenties, had grown up in a lower SES urban ghetto environ-

ment. All were training to become teachers in such a setting. The translating took place over a period of four weeks during meetings with the senior investigator. Translations were made separately and independently by each of the translators; any conflicts were resolved jointly. This procedure resulted in 112 BE concepts.[4]

2. Adjective-elicitation procedure. The 112 concepts were presented to 100 black adolescents attending school in Trenton, New Jersey (median age, 16). The instructions required the Ss to give the most common adjective that they might use "on the street" with each noun. The instructions suggested that the subjects might find it convenient to use a sentence completion format (e.g., "A crib is _____" or "The _____ crib") as an aid to their selection. The testers were black males, and the instructions that they gave to the Ss stressed that the adjectives used should be those likely to be used by the "black and beautiful people."

3. Adjective selection. It should be obvious that the potential number of possibly unique adjectives is quite large ($112 \times 100 = 11,200$). In such a case there would be no basis for selection among the adjectives, and scale construction would be manifestly impossible. In order to determine the extent of commonality, the data were subjected to a special analysis, the same used by Osgood (1971). This analysis selects the most common and unique adjectives among the total set using the following three criteria: salience (total frequency of usage across all nouns), diversity (number of different nouns with which used), and independence (lack of correlation with other adjectives across nouns). Arbitrarily, we selected the highest 60 adjectives resulting from this analysis as providing the initial version of the lower SES black semantic differential, hereafter referred to as the BSD.

4. Opposite selection. The original group of translators was called together and asked to provide the opposites for the 60 adjectives se-

[4] The reader may have noticed and wondered how or why we arrived at 112 BP concepts starting with only 100 nouns taken from the studies of Osgood and his associates. The explanation is simple. As so often happens, consensus among 10 individuals was an elusive goal, and a few irreconcilable differences in translations remained. When two translations of the same AE noun both had a substantial number of proponents, both translations were included. When the same translation was given to two AE nouns, the translated BP noun was presented to the subjects with the appropriate AE noun in parentheses.

We wish to express our appreciation to R. M. Slivka, then of the New Jersey Urban Schools Development Council, for his help in the translation and adjective-elicitation phases of the present study.

lected in step 3. Again, the emphasis was on the opposites that would be used in everyday street conversation. The 60 adjectives and their opposites are shown in Table 1.

5. Concept-on-scale procedure. Twelve booklets were prepared, each comprising a random set of 10 of 112 concepts. (The twelfth booklet contained the remaining two concepts plus eight concepts randomly selected from the first 110.) Each concept was to be rated on each of the 60 BSD scales. In constructing the booklets, the 60 scales were randomized on a page in terms of order as well as position (left versus right) of the "positive" end of the scale. Each booklet then consisted of 20 pages (two pages for each concept, with each page containing 30 scales). Additionally, the 12 booklets were duplicated with reversed scale order, producing a total of 24 booklets. Each of the test booklets was then administered to at least 20 black adolescent pupils in the ghetto area of the West Side of Chicago. Although it was originally planned that each *S* would complete an entire booklet (that is, make a total of 600 judgments), this proved impractical given school time constraints and a high absentee rate at test sites. Therefore, each *S* completed the rating of at least one concept on all 60 scales. Some, of course, did more. This procedural modification resulted in 760 *S*s participating in the data gathering.

Our original plan had been to carry the entire project out in Trenton, New Jersey. However, just after the elicitation phase, Trenton went through a period of school disruption centering around an interracial busing plan. The resulting residue of racial feelings made it impractical, if not impossible, to continue in that school district. Our colleague, Professor Savage, was at that time located in Chicago. He, and his colleagues examined the adjectives and it was their opinion that no significant deviation was apparent between the "Trenton" set and those that might be gathered from Chicago teen-agers. We proceeded on this basis. The cleanness of the factor analysis (see below) indicates that this decision was not imprudent.

ANALYSIS OF THE DATA

Black Semantic Differential

Factor analysis: The data were cast in the form of a 60×112 matrix, with the cell entries being the means of all judgments made of the given concept on the given scale. This matrix was then subjected to a

Table 1 Black Semantic Differential Scales

hep	:	:	:	:	:	:	dumb
fast	:	:	:	:	:	:	slow
straight	:	:	:	:	:	:	stone
brave	:	:	:	:	:	:	punk
rotten	:	:	:	:	:	:	cool
ferocious	:	:	:	:	:	:	peaceful
square	:	:	:	:	:	:	straight
passive	:	:	:	:	:	:	active
chump	:	:	:	:	:	:	powerful
badly	:	:	:	:	:	:	uptight
wrong	:	:	:	:	:	:	together
funny	:	:	:	:	:	:	dry
together	:	:	:	:	:	:	sick
weird	:	:	:	:	:	:	straight
light action	:	:	:	:	:	:	dangerous
angular	:	:	:	:	:	:	rounded
slim	:	:	:	:	:	:	phat (fat)
dizzy	:	:	:	:	:	:	together
hep	:	:	:	:	:	:	young
dumb	:	:	:	:	:	:	smart
straight	:	:	:	:	:	:	high
soft	:	:	:	:	:	:	hard
straight	:	:	:	:	:	:	hard up
red	:	:	:	:	:	:	dark
hip	:	:	:	:	:	:	lousy
silly	:	:	:	:	:	:	cool
dry	:	:	:	:	:	:	hip
nasty	:	:	:	:	:	:	clean
warm	:	:	:	:	:	:	cool
ragged	:	:	:	:	:	:	sharp
wide	:	:	:	:	:	:	frail
mellow	:	:	:	:	:	:	yellow
thick	:	:	:	:	:	:	thin
good	:	:	:	:	:	:	foul
honest	:	:	:	:	:	:	slick
black	:	:	:	:	:	:	white
lay	:	:	:	:	:	:	get
slow	:	:	:	:	:	:	heavy
broke	:	:	:	:	:	:	loaded
big	:	:	:	:	:	:	small
tense	:	:	:	:	:	:	relaxed
straight	:	:	:	:	:	:	jive
low	:	:	:	:	:	:	high
terrible	:	:	:	:	:	:	chump
jam	:	:	:	:	:	:	bad scene
dufus	:	:	:	:	:	:	hipped
rich	:	:	:	:	:	:	cheap
large	:	:	:	:	:	:	small

Table 1 (Continued)

out___	:___	:___	:___	:___	:___	:___	in
cool___	:___	:___	:___	:___	:___	:___	uptight
lame___	:___	:___	:___	:___	:___	:___	smooth
soul brother___	:___	:___	:___	:___	:___	:___	tom
big___	:___	:___	:___	:___	:___	:___	little
loose___	:___	:___	:___	:___	:___	:___	tight
dull___	:___	:___	:___	:___	:___	:___	sharp
crooked___	:___	:___	:___	:___	:___	:___	straight
free___	:___	:___	:___	:___	:___	:___	tied down
hot___	:___	:___	:___	:___	:___	:___	cold
all right___	:___	:___	:___	:___	:___	:___	mad
straight___	:___	:___	:___	:___	:___	:___	beat

principal-components factor analysis; six factors extracted were rotated to the Varimax approximation of simple structure. Only the first three factors, which account for 52% of the variance, are used in later analysis. Table 2 presents the loadings of the four highest-loading scales on each of the three primary factors.

Semantic profiles: The mean ratings of each concept on scales marking each of the factors shown in Table 2 were computed. These means were then standardized to permit comparisons between concepts, scales, and another population of subjects (see below). Table 3 gives the standardized composite ratings for each of the 112 BP and 100 AE concepts on the three factors.

American English Data

These data, gathered in 1961-62, were subjected to analyses which were identical to those described above. The scales used to obtain the standardized composite AE ratings (in Table 3) are given in Table 4.

Table 2 Black Semantic Differential Scales Used to Tap Evaluation, Potency, and Activity

Evaluation	Potency	Activity
good–foul (.88)[a]	large–small (.84)	active–passive (.79)
all right–mad (.86)	big–small (.83)	free–tied down (.59)
hard up–straight (.85)	big–little (.80)	fast–slow (.57)
peaceful–ferocious (.85)	wide–frail (.54)	loose–tight (.57)

[a] Numbers in parentheses are factor loadings after Varimax rotation.

Table 3 Standardized Composite Ratings for the 100 AE Concepts and the Corresponding 112 BP Concepts on the Primary EPA Factors

	E	P	A
CRIB	1.160	.253	.157
HOUSE	.427	.465	−.951
SISTER (GIRL)	1.234	−1.751	1.728
SISTER (GIRL) (W-1973)	.580	−.322	.297
GIRL	1.044	−2.476	1.106
GIRL (B-1973)	−.023	−.452	−.158
FLICK	−.153	.020	.926
PICTURE	.633	−.897	−.720
TIGHT (TRUST)	.475	−.419	.086
(TRUST) (W-1973)	.986	.660	−.134
TRUST	.730	1.114	−.951
TRUST (B-1973)	.161	.098	−.271
HURT	−1.963	−.054	−1.105
(RAIN) *	—	—	—
DONE IN	−2.056	−1.550	−1.984
DEFEAT	−1.973	−.292	−.573
BOOK	1.172	.959	1.102
BOOK	.341	.271	−.636
BET	−.175	.046	−.353
(BOOK) *	—	—	—
WATER	.562	.786	.454
WATER	.438	−.357	−.405
GIG	.062	.157	−.397
GIG (WORK) (W-1973)	.682	−.009	−.040
WORK	−.351	.660	.267
WORK (B-1973)	−.252	−.587	−.257
LIE	−1.409	−.815	−.946
(STORY) *	—	—	—
GROUNDED	−.218	−1.264	−1.160
PUNISHMENT	−1.476	.422	−.132

Note: Order of concept presentation is as follows: BP concepts appear first, singly or in parentheses, and AE concepts appear last.

* Indicates AE concept which, when translated, produced a BP word not comparable in meaning to original AE meaning. In such cases the standardized composite AE scores are not presented.

+ Indicates inclusion of BP concept not produced by translation from original AE concept. In such cases standardized composite scores are presented because AE and BP meanings are comparable.

Table 3 (Continued)

	E	P	A
BROAD (WOMAN)	−.346	−.958	1.135
BROAD (WOMAN) (W-1973)	.044	−.270	.267
WOMAN	.752	−2.411	1.715
WOMAN (B-1973)	−.170	−.557	−.334
(CLOUD)+	.391	−.207	−.908
CLOUD	.579	−.357	−1.455
CAT	−.346	−1.603	.322
MAN	.060	.054	.918
DUDE	.149	−1.286	−.390
BROTHER	.992	1.283	2.266
DUDE (MAN) (W-1973)	−.357	.155	.179
MAN	.060	.054	.918
MAN (B-1973)	−.519	−.232	−.276
POISON	−1.596	−1.323	−1.319
POISON	−2.297	.098	−1.740
CRIME	−2.069	.242	−1.308
CRIME	−2.557	.141	.225
STARVING	−1.863	−1.328	−2.280
HUNGER	−1.919	−1.481	−.489
OUT OF SIGHT	.976	.385	2.233
(CHOICE) *	—	—	—
STATIC	−1.565	−1.476	.672
(NOISE) *	—	—	—
WANT	.450	−.107	.262
WANT (W-1973)	−.421	.094	−.180
NEED	−.334	.422	.225
NEED (B-1973)	−.381	−.267	−.187
PISSED OFF	−2.258	−1.116	−1.259
ANGER	−2.427	.638	.960
KISS	1.844	2.071	.448
(TONGUE) *	—	—	—
RAP	.839	1.706	1.003
TALK		(not in original AE)	
H.	−.784	−.059	−.875
(HORSE) *	—	—	—

Table 3 (Continued)

	E	P	A
MARRIED	.615	.268	.635
MARRIAGE	1.217	1.027	.645
CON	−1.440	−.641	.410
CON (W-1973)	−.693	−.386	−.174
GAME	−.081	.184	1.736
GAME (B-1973)	−.276	−.378	−.377
COLOR	1.007	.274	1.195
COLOR	.438	−.811	.006
HEART (COURAGE)	1.004	1.024	1.212
COURAGE	.546	1.027	.414
PARTNER	.920	.305	.921
FRIEND	.676	.984	1.694
DIED ⎱	−.560	−.413	−2.099
WASTED ⎰	−1.552	−1.127	−1.319
DEATH	−1.367	−.811	−2.714
HEAVY (KNOWLEDGEABLE)	.743	1.077	1.299
HEAVY (KNOWLEDGEABLE) (W-1973)	.357	.414	−.053
KNOWLEDGE	.773	1.979	−.069
FREEDOM	.594	.924	1.025
FREEDOM	1.124	2.130	.813
YOUR BAG	.936	.374	.844
YOUR BAG (W-1973)	.548	.370	.139
BELIEF	.860	1.741	.246
BELIEF (B-1973)	−.008	.047	−.299
MADE IT	1.013	−.260	.383
SUCCESS	.363	.530	.309
(ROPE)+	.136	−.646	−.880
ROPE	−.578	.033	−1.035
z's	.214	−.191	.597
SLEEP	1.055	−.400	−.888
FUTURE	1.013	1.732	1.519
FUTURE	.611	.335	.540
EGG (FOOD)	.699	−1.169	−.265
FOOD	.849	.184	−.993
ROOT	.121	−.028	−.309
ROOT	−.059	.271	−.363

Table 3 (Continued)

	E	P	A
(SUN)+	.391	2.219	−.457
SUN	.838	2.325	−.951
DOG (ANIMAL)	−.887	−.440	.734
DOG	.071	.033	2.303
LOW-LIFE	−1.145	−2.792	−2.209
(DOG) *	—	—	—
POT (MARIJUANA)	−1.185	.189	−.447
(SMOKE) *	—	—	—
CHUMP	−.927	−2.961	−1.111
(FISH) *	—	—	—
DUKES	.049	.036	.284
HAND	.146	.422	.624
OLD LADY (MOTHER)	.982	−.524	.135
OLD LADY (MOTHER) (W-1973)	.436	−.240	−.316
MOTHER	1.011	−.248	.267
MOTHER (B-1973)	.310	−.207	−.100
KNOT	−.097	−1.180	−.666
KNOT	−.621	−.184	−1.035
LIFE	−.189	.231	.750
LIFE	.417	.703	1.295
SKULL	.112	.015	−.584
HEAD	.244	−.032	.477
(THUNDER)+	−1.167	2.002	.328
THUNDER	−1.270	1.092	.750
FOR REAL	.936	.707	.393
FOR REAL (W-1973)	.167	.020	−.136
TRUTH	.568	1.092	−.279
TRUTH (B-1973)	−.106	−.268	−.135
WRITER	.541	.290	.783
AUTHOR	.017	−.292	−.006
SOUNDS	1.446	.575	1.470
MUSIC	.644	.141	.498
WEDNESDAY	.062	−.413	−.468
WEDNESDAY	−.265	−.703	−.300

Table 3 (Continued)

	E	P	A
SEAT	.255	.829	−1.067
CHAIR	.406	−.465	−1.245
QUILT	.600	.068	−.705
(——) *	—	—	—
LUCK	.441	−.598	.157
LUCK	.503	−1.221	.183
(PEACE)+	.954	−.699	−.419
PEACE	1.033	−.292	.267
KINKY	−.240	−.635	−.117
AFRO	1.380	1.331	1.365
HAIR	.211	−2.216	.162
BREAD (FOOD)	.727	.110	−1.188
(FOOD)+	.824	.813	.146
TO GREEZE	−.128	.559	−.007
FOOD	.849	.184	−.993
(SEED)+	.068	−.694	−1.281
SEED	.308	−1.805	−.258
PIG (POLICEMAN)	−.993	−.836	−1.627
PIG (POLICEMAN) (W-1973)	−.817	.278	.089
THE MAN	−.408	.533	.399
THE MAN (POLICEMAN) (W-1973)	−.727	.087	−.121
POLICEMAN	−.232	−.638	1.044
POLICEMAN (B-1973)	−.940	−.147	.146
UPTIGHT	−.570	−.931	−.227
FEAR	−2.135	−.443	−.657
OLD MAN	1.017	.829	.503
OLD MAN (W-1973)	−.024	−.155	−.361
FATHER	.752	−.097	.456
FATHER (B-1973)	−.179	−.352	−.428
GROOVY	1.188	.601	2.101
PLEASURE	.925	.054	.855
PROGRAM	.335	.290	.454
YOUR THING	1.396	1.563	1.431
PURPOSE	.254	−.097	.519
(FIRE)+	−2.009	1.632	.432
FIRE	−1.627	.768	1.274

Table 3 (Continued)

	E	P	A
(DOCTOR) +	.886	.892	.558
DOCTOR	.752	.119	.477
STRENGTH	.233	1.368	1.063
POWER	−.027	1.503	1.023
WINDOW	−.075	−.334	−1.061
WINDOW	.481	−1.697	−1.203
STAR	1.352	2.007	1.008
STAR	.860	.379	−2.294
BREAD (MONEY)	.634	1.304	.717
MONEY	.654	.898	−.573
FRUIT (FOOD) +	1.222	.617	−.985
FRUIT	.698	−1.027	−.510
(BIRD [ANIMAL]) +	−.454	−.900	.130
BIRD	.157	−2.065	1.778
FAG	−1.624	−1.862	−1.512
(FRUIT) *	—	—	—
T-BIRD WINE	−.178	−1.127	−.156
(BIRD) *	—	—	—
LOW-DOWN DUDE	−1.773	−1.222	−1.089
(SNAKE) *	—	—	—
GUN	−1.182	.728	.223
(HEAT) *	—	—	—
LAYOUT	.021	−.308	.015
MAP	−.081	−1.243	−1.182
OLD MAN (HUSBAND) (W-1973)	.211	−1.190	−.820
OLD MAN (HUSBAND) (W-1973)	−.229	−.240	−.121
HUSBAND	.352	.314	1.421
HUSBAND (B-1973)	−.101	−.521	−.365
(RAIN [WATER]) +	.242	−.916	1.206
RAIN	.244	−.681	.246
(TREE) +	.681	1.230	−2.401
TREE	−.113	.357	−.153
DRUNK (ON LIQUOR)	−1.338	−.371	.322
(STONE) *	—	—	—

Table 3 (Continued)

	E	P	A
HIGH (ON "POT")	− .968	.570	− .145
(STONE) *	—	—	—
(RESPECT)⁺	1.318	.168	.295
RESPECT	1.011	1.006	− .993
EAR	1.017	− .720	− .221
EAR	.427	−1.567	.372
CRACK UP	−1.095	− .218	− .649
(LAUGHTER) *	—	—	—
(MOON)⁺	.550	.501	− .705
MOON	.654	.681	−2.861
SUPER-NIGGER	.195	.115	.783
(STAR) *	—	—	—
FIGHT	−1.885	− .271	− .496
BATTLE	−2.373	1.006	.456
TROUBLE	−1.549	− .001	−1.243
DANGER	−2.178	.746	.216
I CAN DIG IT	.939	.765	1.552
I CAN DIG IT (SYMPATHY) (W-1973)	.679	.143	− .076
SYMPATHY	.752	− .313	− .552
SYMPATHY (B-1973)	− .281	− .209	− .451
MOVING UP	.609	.691	.964
MOVING UP (PROGRESS) (W-1973)	.219	.046	.224
PROGRESS	.222	.811	.561
PROGRESS (B-1973)	− .197	− .147	− .243
CUP	.824	− .022	− .924
CUP	.406	−1.546	−1.098
HEART	1.007	.274	1.195
COURAGE	.546	1.027	.414
CROOK	−1.646	− .509	− .007
CROOK (W-1973)	− .871	− .212	.283
LIBERATOR	.258	.020	.657
LIBERATOR (W-1973 [THIEF])	− .557	− .459	.235
THIEF	−2.546	− .983	.015
THIEF (B-1973)	− .684	− .071	− .264
NOSE IS OPENED	− .187	− .408	− .853
LOVE	1.228	.984	.157
LOVE (B-1973)	.133	− .046	− .153

Table 3 (Continued)

	E	P	A
HAWK ⎫ BREEZE⎬	−1.639	−.022	−.573
	.391	.068	.218
WIND	−.102	.811	.477
RIVER	−.293	1.584	.734
RIVER	.168	.725	−.762
(CAT [ANIMAL])+	−.032	−1.143	1.140
CAT	−.492	−1.805	1.526

Table 4 American English Semantic Differential Scales

Evaluation	Potency	Activity
awful–nice	strong–weak	noisy–quiet
sour–sweet	powerful–powerless	young–old
hellish–heavenly	big–little	slow–fast
good–bad	shallow–deep	alive–dead

Interpretation of the Factors

The three AE factors have already been identified as representing Evaluation, Potency, and Activity. With regard to the BP data, it is clear that Factors II and III represent Potency and Activity respectively. It is also clear that Factor I has a strong evaluative component. While there may be other aspects tapped by Factor I, the parallels are clear enough to permit it to be labeled Evaluation.

ADDITIONAL DATA

The BP data presented in Table 3 were gathered in 1971; the AE data were obtained in 1961. Each used different scales and predominantly different concepts. This, of course, was within the original research design and consistent with the strictures of cross-cultural research. However, problems arise when one attempts to make unambiguous interpretations of the differences that are presented in Table 3.

The difficulties arise from two sources. First, the ten-year time span between the two sets of data may cause some interpretative mischief — the decade between 1961 and 1971 was extremely volatile both politically and culturally. In particular, many of the feelings of white middle-class youth about the "establishment" *may* have changed because of the Viet Nam war. Certainly the involvement of youth and the rise of white radical movements in demonstrations against the war and other perceived social inequities would lead one to suspect that such a conclusion is warranted. Thus white youth in 1971 may have moved considerably closer to black youth than was true in 1961.

Second, where different concepts (e.g., PIG [BP] and POLICEMAN [AE]) were presented to the two groups, we do not know whether the differences in EPA profiles are due to real differences in meaning of the underlying concepts or to different interpretations of the two stimuli. Put another way, is the referent of PIG and POLICEMAN exactly the same within the two populations? If not, then the interpretation of differences for the cases where different concepts were rated has to be made with some care.

In order to check on these possibilities, a second study was conducted. Thirty-three male (17 black and 16 white) lower classmen at Governors State University were presented with a set of concepts from the other racial group. That is, the white subjects rated a set of BP concepts, while the black subjects were given the AE concepts. Each rated the concepts on a 12-scale semantic differential, the scales of which were the same used to compute the standardized scores in Table 3. These data were converted to standard scores (separately for E, P, and A), and the results are also presented in Table 3, with the race of the subjects and the year of data gathering (i.e., B-1973) indicated.

The Governors State students should not be taken to represent a sample equivalent to the 1971 Chicago group. The original sample was probably much more lower class than the college students. However, the character of the university, which attracts students whose backgrounds have been more work-oriented (as opposed to classroom-focused), would lead one to believe that this sample falls somewhere between the 1971 group and samples of blacks that one would find at more traditional universities. This speculation is supported by the data in Table 3, where we find that the college students often occupy a middle position between the 1961 and 1971 samples.

RESULTS AND DISCUSSION

Inspection of Table 3 reveals many concepts in which differences among the groups appear. In fact, there are far too many differences for us to discuss them adequately here. Therefore, the majority of the data will be presented as empirical findings without further discussion. Those aspects which we will examine are within that subset dealing with the respondent's perception of the outside world — that is, those which bear upon the level of "eco-system distrust."

In interpreting the differences between the standardized scores given in Table 3, the reader may view a difference value of .64 as significant at the .05 level. This value is derived assuming that there was an average N of 20 in each group contributing to a given rating, and that the mean of the distribution of standard scores is equal to 0 with a standard deviation of 1.0.

In line with our orientation to the conceptualization of eco-system distrust, we shall discuss concepts falling into four categories: material possessions, confrontation, personal relations, and quality of life. It should be pointed out that by explicitly dealing with less than 25% of the data, we are doing little more than highlighting the findings.

MATERIAL POSSESSIONS

Two concepts fit into this category: HOUSE (AE), CRIB (BP), and MONEY (AE), BREAD (BP). HOUSE is a concept that is very positively evaluated by blacks and is neutral for whites. (It would be "good" for blacks to have a house.) No difference appears on the Potency dimension; both groups rate it neutral. On Activity there is a significant difference with the concept being neutral for blacks and inactive for whites.

In the case of MONEY, blacks do not evaluate the concept any more positively than do whites. However, blacks do see the concept as being more active (perhaps owing to a perception of having to work harder for it).

In general, it would seem that with regard to the two concepts representing material possessions, blacks want the same things that whites do. But blacks also realize that these things are not as easy for them to obtain, and investing these items with too much wishful energy may be more hopeless than helpful.

CONFRONTATION

We placed, rather arbitrarily, seven concepts in this category: CRIME (AE), CRIME (BP); THIEF (AE), CROOK (BP), LIBERATOR (BP); POLICEMAN (AE), PIG (BP), THE MAN (BP); DEFEAT (AE), DONE-IN (BP); BATTLE (AE), FIGHT (BP); GAME (AE), CON (BP); and DANGER (AE), TROUBLE (BP).

Let us consider first the concept CRIME. Blacks and whites consider CRIME as being very "bad" and of neutral Potency. Blacks see it as significantly much more inactive than whites. We can, perhaps, interpret the data to indicate that blacks are as repelled by crime as whites but are often helpless in preventing its occurrence or consequences. Being an urban black implies an existence in closer environmental proximity to crime.

With regard to the perpetrators of crime (i.e., THIEF), there were two translations given: CROOK and LIBERATOR. In the original data for blacks CROOK appears to be closer in meaning to what the whites meant by the term THIEF. Blacks view CROOK as somewhat negative and weak, while LIBERATOR was positive and active, thus presenting a positive picture, perhaps because of the ideological implications of the concept. To the extent that the same person viewed as a THIEF by whites is seen as a LIBERATOR by blacks makes the task of crime prevention more complex and difficult.

Perhaps the most significant difference between the widely differing black and white evaluation of these three concepts in the original data and the 1973 evaluations is the *lack* of significant differences in both black and white reactions to CROOK, THIEF, and LIBERATOR in the 1973 data. Blacks and whites in 1973 evaluate the three negatively, but the extremes of the earlier data are not found. Interestingly, LIBERATOR tends toward the least negative evaluation even though whites were the respondents to this concept.

Consider the original EPA ratings for persons concerned with law enforcement: POLICEMAN, THE MAN, PIG. Again, between the two translations given, THE MAN seems closer to the white meaning than PIG. However, THE MAN is seen to be significantly less active than POLICEMAN. This may reflect the feeling that the police do very little in the ghetto to protect the residents. This feeling is more strongly shown in the ratings of the concept PIG. This concept is seen not only as significantly worse on E than the white rating but also as being quite impotent and inactive. Again, the implications for institutional change are obvious and need not be belabored here.

The 1973 evaluation of PIG and THE MAN shows a similarity of white respondents to the original blacks' strongly negative evaluation of PIG. POLICEMAN for 1973 blacks is as strongly negative as was PIG for the original blacks. Whites in 1973 consider PIG slightly potent and neutral on Activity, still a contrast to the strong impotent and inactive ratings given by blacks in the original data. Considering the remaining 1973 rating of THE MAN and POLICEMAN, black and white views are not very far either positively or negatively from neutral.

GAME-CON are placed in this category rather arbitrarily in as much as CON seems to have a strongly negative and socially disapproved rating in the original data. The blacks responded to CON as significantly less good, less potent, and less active than did whites. These differences may be more understandable if we translate CON to CONGAME.

The 1973 data on these concepts reinforce the evidence of similarity of views between blacks and whites noted in the previous discussion of 1973 data. Ratings of CON and GAME on E, P, and A by blacks and whites in 1973 are strikingly similar and less extreme than the original ratings. Whether this is more reflective of the reduction of confounding variables inherent in the comparison in the original data between groups of subjects differing in social class, geographic location, and time, or more reflective of greater actual similarity between views held by blacks and whites in 1973, remains to be investigated.

The final three concepts in this category all deal with negative events that might happen to someone. Blacks see DANGER-TROUBLE as less negative, more impotent, and more inactive in contrast to the white response. Again, part of the explanation may be the feeling of being unprotected from TROUBLE; it is a fact of ghetto experience out of one's control.

The other two concepts, BATTLE-FIGHT and DEFEAT–DONE-IN, show a pattern similar to DANGER. Presumably the same interpretation would obtain.

PERSONAL RELATIONS

Six concepts are placed in this category: BELIEF (AE), YOUR BAG (BP); TRUTH (AE), FOR REAL (BP); RESPECT (AE), RESPECT (BP);

LOVE (AE), NOSE IS OPENED (BP); TRUST (AE), TIGHT (BP); and SYMPATHY (AE), I CAN DIG IT (BP).

In the original data TRUTH is valued somewhat more by blacks than whites, is less potent, and is more active. However, with the exception of the Activity scale, the differences may not be significant. The ratings may indicate that blacks feel that TRUTH is something that has to be actively sought after — it is not a fact of life. In the 1973 data there are no significant differences in this concept between blacks and whites on E, P, or A, and the ratings again are fairly close to neutral.

RESPECT follows a pattern quite similar to TRUTH. Here the Potency and Activity differences are significant. These data may mean that while RESPECT, for blacks, is something important to have, it has little power to change one's life, and at the same time it is not something that can be taken for granted in interpersonal relations.

TRUST in the original data follows a pattern similar to the prior two concepts, with the exception of a somewhat lower E value. The data suggest that TRUST is something to be given cautiously and not as a matter of course in relationships with others. When we compare the original data with those gathered in 1973, some interesting differences appear. On Evaluation the original whites rate TRUST more positively than do the original blacks, but the difference is not significant. There are significant differences in the Evaluation of TRUST between whites and blacks in 1973, however, because 1973 blacks value TRUST *less* than the original blacks. In Potency and Activity, however, the 1973 respondents' ratings of TRUST are fairly close together and lie between the extremes of the original black and white ratings.

SYMPATHY, on the other hand, presents quite a different picture. It is a comparatively potent and quietly active concept for blacks. These data suggest that having SYMPATHY is likely to lead to changes in a black relationship; being sympathetic means sharing a level of understanding about life's problems which is unavailable to outsiders. The neutral (Potency) and inactive ratings given this concept by whites may reflect a perception that SYMPATHY has relatively little impact on daily life.

The 1973 data on SYMPATHY in some ways parallel the 1973 findings for TRUST. Where in the original data SYMPATHY is evaluated positively by both blacks and whites, in 1973 blacks rate it negatively and whites rate it positively, and the difference is significant. In Potency and Activity the ratings are slightly negative and are closer to the original white ratings. The 1973 black and white and the original white ratings of SYMPATHY are all significantly different from the strongly positive Potency and Activity ratings of the original blacks.

The two groups of the original data evaluate BELIEF quite similarly, but blacks consider it less potent and more active. Perhaps these data imply that, for blacks, while beliefs may be held, they are subject to almost continual negative reinforcement. In the 1973 data blacks rate BELIEF as neutral or slightly negative on E, P, and A. Whites rate YOUR BAG positively on the three factors, but the ratings are not significantly different from 1973 black ratings.

Finally, we consider LOVE. This concept, the basis of a state which, ideally, requires TRUST, SYMPATHY, and RESPECT, is viewed by blacks as significantly less good, less potent, and less active compared to the ratings by the white sample. Before we make much out of the differences in ratings, we should be aware that blacks usually use NOSE IS OPENED to denote a vulnerable condition somewhat akin to romantic infatuation, and one in which the infatuated person expects and is expected to be taken advantage of.

There is only black 1973 data on LOVE. On Evaluation and Potency the scores are very close to original black ratings. Original black and 1973 ratings are significantly less positive than original white ratings on Evaluation and Potency. On Activity, however, 1973 black ratings are close to original white ratings and are significantly less negative than original black ratings.

QUALITY OF LIFE

We placed ten concepts in this category: WORK (AE), GIG (BP); PROGRESS (AE), MOVING UP (BP); HOPE (AE), HOPE (BP); SUCCESS (AE), MADE IT (BP); FUTURE (AE), FUTURE (BP); MARRIAGE (AE), MARRIAGE (BP); FREEDOM (AE), FREEDOM (BP); LIFE (AE), LIFE (BP); LUCK (AE), LUCK (BP); and PEACE (AE), PEACE (BP).

First, let us consider MARRIAGE. Blacks consider MARRIAGE to be less good and less potent than whites. In a society where the possibilities to fulfill the responsibilities of a good marriage (e.g., economic security, provision of a good life for one's children) are limited, these data should not be surprising.

Work presents some interesting and important differences. For whites, work is somewhat negatively evaluated; blacks see the concept as neutral. For blacks, however, work is less potent and less active than for whites. These data may be interpreted to indicate that while blacks value work as much as, if not more than, do whites, it is a less functionally relevant concept to them, possibly because it is more difficult to obtain for a lower SES black. There is a widely held stereotype that blacks have a low motivation for work. It is difficult to reconcile that stereotype with data that show blacks valuing work somewhat more than do whites.

In 1973 whites evaluate work positively, significantly more so than both whites in the original data and blacks in 1973. Work is considered neutral to negative on Potency and Activity by 1973 respondents, and is significantly less potent for 1973 respondents than for white respondents in the original data.

Under normal circumstances (i.e., the white world) work leads to progress. Thus at the same time that blacks were neutral on work, they also gave higher evaluative ratings to progress as well as somewhat higher Activity ratings. Progress probably includes (for blacks) more than advancing within a work setting. These differences, while in a consistent direction, are not statistically significant.

The 1973 blacks rated progress negatively on E, P, and A; whites rated it positively on all three factors though the differences between white and black 1973 ratings were not significant. Significant differences between 1973 and original ratings were several: 1973 blacks evaluated progress significantly less positively than the original blacks; all 1973 subjects considered it significantly less potent than all original subjects; and 1973 blacks considered it significantly less active than the original respondents. One might speculate that the 1973 ratings indicate a *general* disillusionment or even cynicism where progress is concerned.

The belief that success is a good thing is significantly stronger among blacks than among whites. At the same time this is a relatively neutral concept, indicating perhaps that blacks see success as more difficult to obtain than whites do.

We now come to a set of very abstract concepts in which the differences between the groups are not statistically significant. HOPE is good, but less so for the blacks than the whites. Perhaps this may be realistic in a society often perceived as racist and oppressive.

While many of the interpretations presented above give a picture of the black view of American life that to some seems depressing, to others, realistic, the ratings of the concept FUTURE are more encouraging. The significantly more positive ratings on all three dimensions for the blacks may suggest that blacks recognize and anticipate change.

FREEDOM was a concept that our informants refused to translate. They gave the rationale that it was an "irrelevant" concept. From the ratings it is easy to see why. Thus FREEDOM is seen as less positive, neither potent nor impotent (but significantly less so than whites' ratings), and not significantly higher on Activity. It is, in truth, an irrelevant concept.

The scores from both groups on the concept LIFE are parallel, with the blacks being significantly more neutral on two dimensions but positive on A. Again, the interpretation seems to reflect a generally negative view of current life, which nonetheless necessarily involves Activity.

LUCK and PEACE show generally similar patterns between the two groups, although PEACE is significantly less active for blacks. The somewhat more potent ratings given LUCK by the black sample may indicate a belief that chance plays a rather important role in their lives.

AN INVITATION TO THE READER

We have engaged in rather free-reining interpretations of some of our research data, although these interpretations are consistent with the conclusions of other researchers. We have done this primarily to give the reader a flavor of one part of psychological research, the interpretation of data with the goal of finding a consistent pattern in them. The remainder of the data are presented in Table 3. We invite the interested reader to attempt the same process for himself. Thought should be given to probable implications for further research (developing hypotheses), because any such speculations are exploratory and so are *ex post facto*. They need ultimately to be tested by research based on *a priori* predictions. However, the same kind of process can be achieved by looking at the list of BP concepts (Table 3) and, based on a set of theories or assumptions about differences between black and white experience, making predictions about how the concepts might be rated in BP in contrast to AE. Without having to go through the arduous process of data gathering, the reader can then verify his predictions immediately, based on the uninterpreted data in Table 3.

IMPLICATIONS

There are some very perceptive comments on the feelings and perceptions of the black adult male in America in Elliot Liebow's book *Tally's Corner* (1967). He notes, for example, that the black lower-class male seeks out marriage because "... he wants to be publicly, legally married, to support a family and be the head of it because this is what it is to be a man in our society, whether one lives in a room near the carry-out or in an elegant house in the suburbs" (p. 210).

Yet this is a dream which is doomed to be self-destructive. For his personal history, and that of his father and his father before him, is mired in the failure that any black man reaching his majority since 1865 knows only too well. These men have to be skeptical of the possibilities of reaching their dream — they can see the barriers to these dreams all around them.

Our feeling from the data presented in the previous pages is that not only do blacks value the same goals, relationships, and ideals that whites do, but in many cases they value them more. Where the differences occur, they seem to be related to perceptions of the amount of effort necessary to achieve those goals and the potency of those aims in changing one's life. In other words, blacks want the same things whites do, but they don't believe that (a) they can achieve them, (b) if they could, their lives would be significantly improved, and (c) they would be engaged in anything less than a constant struggle to maintain those things they do achieve.

Another suggestion in the data concerns interpersonal relationships. The NORC study mentioned elsewhere in this book (NORC, February, 1963) suggests that blacks find it more difficult than whites to place trust in others. Not only is this verified here, but the level of trust has actually decreased over the period 1971-73. Of more importance is the evident feeling that being trusting, while good in itself, is dangerous because whites have historically mishandled the trust of blacks.

There is an aura of being a victim which comes through in the data — or at least it seems so to the present authors. We allude to the belief that one is relatively unprotected from trouble, danger, and defeat. These are realities of life which social protectors (e.g., parents) and institutions are unlikely to do anything about. It may be the recognition of these perceptions of lack of control that have led various bodies to demand local control of public institutions, as a mechanism for reducing the level of eco-system distrust by giving to blacks a sense of being in control of their own destinies.

The hypotheses in the prior paragraphs receive some support from a *post hoc* analysis of the data in Table 3. It was reasoned that if blacks exhibited higher levels of eco-system distrust, then they should generally give lower EPA ratings to those concepts which might be related to such levels. A Wilcoxon signed-ranks test was performed on a subset of the concepts.[5] The results indicated support for the hypothesis on Evaluation ($Z = 1.75, p = .04$, one tailed) and Potency ($Z = 2.19, p = .01$, one tailed). While the test was negative for Activity, a sign test performed on these data indicated a consistent tendency to rate the concepts as being less active ($Z = 2.01, p = .02$, one tailed). Since an analysis over all concepts and dimensions in Table 3 did not produce significant differences, it would seem that the differences reported above are not due to a general response set.

The findings of significant differences in direction and magnitude over all three dimensions (with the exception of Activity) extends the concept of eco-system distrust. The greater significance of the difference of Potency suggests that a feeling of impotence about the environment and critical persons may possibly underlie the lack of trust. Such a finding is certainly consonant with the reports of perceptive observers (e.g., Liebow, 1967) of the black urban scene.

While the general picture with regard to immediate events, institutions, persons, and psychological states is rather depressing, and becoming even more so, one can take some solace in the finding that blacks are positively oriented toward the future. However, before one becomes Candidian about the future and bases public policy on these data, it is well to remember that the future is just that — something

---

[5] The concepts that were used for this test are (in AE form): HOUSE, TRUST, DEFEAT, WORK, WOMAN, NEED, ANGER, MARRIAGE, GAME, DEATH, FREEDOM, MOTHER, LIFE, TRUTH, LUCK, PEACE, POLICEMAN, MONEY, HUSBAND, SYMPATHY, CROOK, and LOVE.

which is yet to come. And it may never come if the present is not altered and the dream becomes reality.

> What happens to a dream deferred?
> Does it dry up like a raisin in the sun?
> Or fester like a sore —
>   and then run?
> Does it stink like rotten meat?
> Or crust and sugar over —
>   like a syrupy sweet?
> Maybe it just sags
>   like a heavy load.
> *Or does it explode?*
>   Langston Hughes (1944)

CHAPTER FIVE

Method and a Sample of Results

H. C. TRIANDIS, R. S. MALPASS,
AND J. FELDMAN

The present chapter is designed for the specialist who wants to know about the methods of data collection and analysis which are the bases of the remaining chapters. It assumes a high level of familiarity with the methodology of the social sciences and with multivariate procedures. Readers who are not interested in these matters may skip this chapter without missing any of the results and conclusions of the study.

OVERALL STRATEGY

The overall strategy was to select concepts, attributes relevant to these concepts, and samples of subjects that would be representative of the kinds of concepts, attributes, and subjects that economically disadvantaged workers and their supervisors are likely to encounter. The broad theoretical framework is described in detail in Triandis et al., *The Analysis of Subjective Culture* (1972) and is derived from Brunswik's probabilistic functionalism (e.g., Hammond, 1966).

Informants selected to represent contrasting groups were asked to give us attributes that they commonly use in thinking about the concepts to be studied. Later phases of the work used these "elicited attributes" in scales on which subjects could make judgments. A combination of the advantages of the anthropological and psychological approaches was attempted, as discussed in Triandis, Weldon, and Feldman (1974).

While the ideal of probabilistic functionalism would have involved random sampling of subjects, stimuli, and response continua, practical limitations required numerous compromises. Since subjects had to make a very large number of judgments, survey methodology could only be used on a subset of these judgments. To arrive at this subset, we selected different race samples that were both as different from and as similar to each other as we could practically find — white, middle-class student females vs. black, ghetto, unemployed males, and black, lower-class males vs. white, lower-class males. This resulted in four samples: two relatively heterogeneous white and two relatively heterogeneous black. When the data clearly showed a difference between the combined black and white samples, we used it as the basis of a hypothesis that there was a subcultural difference. This was later tested with a representative sample.

The basic approach was to ask subjects to assign a number, between 0 and 9, to an intersection between a *concept* (word, person, role) and an *attribute* (feature of the word, characteristic of the person, appropriateness of a behavior within a role, consequence of a behavior, etc.).

In order to sample the concepts and the attributes in a representative way, we employed tasks requiring 4,600 judgments from each subject. Since the number of judgments is too large to do in a reasonable period of time, and since there is evidence (Triandis et al., *The Analysis of Subjective Culture*, 1972) that highly demographically homogeneous samples make subjective culture judgments with small within-group variance and large between-groups variance, we divided the 4,600 judgments into smaller sets and asked homogeneous samples of subjects to make the judgments. Thus we obtained 20 judgments for each concept-attribute intersection from each of the homogeneous samples of subjects.

From multivariate reductions of the data using three-mode factor analysis and discriminant function analysis, we derived a smaller set of less than 600 judgments, requiring about two hours of subject time to complete, which we then cross-validated with a Chicago sample that systematically varied in race (black and white), sex (male and female), age (18-25 and 35-45), and social class (hardcore unemployed, working class, middle class). This $2 \times 2 \times 2 \times 3$ design, with 10 subjects per cell, required the testing of 240 subjects.

The research program employed three distinct phases for the study of six types of concept-attribute intersections. The six types were:

1. Stereotypes (Is a *mother* intelligent? Always $= 9$; Never $= 0$).

2. Behavioral intentions (Would you *trust* a black policeman? Always = 9; Never = 0).

3. Role perceptions (Is it appropriate for a mother to *hit* her son? Always = 9; Never = 0).

4. Job perceptions (Are *truck drivers* well paid? Extremely well paid = 9; Extremely poorly paid = 0).

5. Antecedents of behaviors (Is learning a trade necessary before *joining a union?* Always = 9; Never = 0).

6. Consequents of behaviors (Is *getting a good job* likely to lead to satisfaction? Always = 9; Never = 0).

To ensure that the concepts and scales to which the subjects were to respond were representative of the kinds of concepts and attributes that are used by people like the samples that we were to test in our main study, we undertook Phase I. Here a sample of concepts, selected for their relevance as suggested by reviews of the previous literature (Triandis, 1974; Triandis and Malpass, 1971) and from discussions at an especially convened conference of experts on race relations, was presented to extreme groups of subjects (black ghetto males and white middle-class females). There is evidence in the literature (see Miller and Dreger, 1973) that these samples are maximally different, since black females do not differ as much from white samples as black males do, and white females are the single best "carriers" of white culture. These samples were first given an open-ended questionnaire and asked to think of attributes of each concept to be used in the formats described above. The most frequently given attributes from each sample were combined to form the list of attributes to be used in Phase II.

In Phase II similar contrast samples judged the 4,600 concept-attribute intersections developed in Phase I. As described previously, numbers from 0 to 9 represented the degree of perceived association between concepts and attributes.

The samples themselves were chosen for maximum heterogeneity. Black ghetto males and white college females represented the cultural extremes, as before. Intermediate samples of lower-class black and white high school males were used to provide a racial contrast, controlling for age, sex, and socioeconomic status. It was felt that if both black samples and both white samples agreed within themselves and responded to particular concept-attribute intersections in racially divergent ways, a difference in racially based subjective culture was likely.

The data were submitted, when appropriate, to three-mode factor analysis (Tucker, 1966). This allowed the determination of consistencies in the responses to the attributes, the concepts, and the points of view found in the four samples of subjects. Discriminant function analyses were also used to find the elements of subjective culture that maximally discriminated among the four samples. The intersections yielding the sharpest contrasts were selected for the third phase.

In Phase III a subset of less than 600 judgments was employed. The sample of subjects was selected according to a $2 \times 2 \times 2 \times 3$ factorial design, with 10 subjects per cell as described above. Multivariate analyses of variance were employed as well as discriminant function analyses to determine which demographic characteristics of the subjects predicted their response to these intersections.

The details of the methodology can be seen in Triandis and Malpass (1970), of Phases I and II in technical reports by Triandis, Feldman, and Harvey (1970, 1971a, b, c), and of Phase III in Triandis, Weldon, and Feldman (1972).

SOME DETAILS OF PHASES I AND II

Four samples of individuals were used in Phases I and II: (1) White female college students; (2) black working-class and lower-class high school males, with a normal I.Q. but academic problems which required their placement in a special program. They were from a southern suburb of Chicago with a large black and lower-class white population; (3) white, and some Spanish-speaking, high school males from the same special program as sample 2; (4) black adult males classified according to OEO criteria as hardcore unemployed, from St. Louis, Missouri.

We considered samples 1 and 4 maximally different, since they differed in race, sex, age, education, marital status, and many other variables. The comparison of these samples indicates the limits of variation of subjective culture. Samples 2 and 3 differed only in race, but unfortunately could not be matched on family income. The white students had more income than the black students.

A pool of 83 white female college students did the 4,600 judgments required in Phase II. Questionnaires were designed so that each intersection was judged by 20 subjects from this pool. A pool of 43 white student respondents gave 20 judgments for each intersection. The 60 black students who constituted the black high school pool also produced about 20 judgments for each of the 4,600 intersections. In St. Louis 40 black ghetto males were employed to obtain the 20 judgments for each intersection.

Both the instructions to the subjects and the concepts used in the studies were "translated" by five black students who had a black ghetto background to "black" English and back-translated into "standard" English. A decentering procedure, as recommended by Werner and Campbell (1970), was employed to modify the original English, until a version that could be translated into black English and back-translated faithfully into its original form was obtained. The final questionnaires employed a decentered version of standard English, because it was determined that almost all our subjects understood it. Furthermore, black English is an oral language and questionnaires in black English look "phony." The decentered version contained words that were familiar to all samples and had a style that was simple and direct.

Before administering the questionnaires of Phase II, we obtained subject responses to a "practice sheet" to familiarize them with the task and to check on their comprehension of it. Approximately 10% of the black samples had to be excused from the task because repeated attempts failed to produce accurate judgments on the practice sheets (see Triandis, Feldman, and Harvey, 1970, p. 14, for details).

Both Phases I and II were administered by assistants of the same race and sex as the subjects. Subjects were paid $2.00 per hour for their work. They were tested in small groups of less than 10 to permit close supervision of the comprehension checks. If a subject did not know a word, he was given a standard definition, prepared ahead of time.

SOME DETAILS OF PHASE III

The data were collected by the University of Illinois Survey Research Laboratory. Interviewers of the same sex and race as the persons studied were employed. The interviewers were trained for 18 hours before going to the field, using standard procedures.

The 240 subjects were presented with a questionnaire in which they were asked to make 573 judgments. Specifically, 128 judgments were relevant to their stereotypes, 105 relevant to behavioral intentions, 120 relevant to role perceptions, 40 on job perceptions, and 90 on antecedents and 90 on consequents of events.

Since the judgments obtained in Phases I and II included all the judgments required in Phase III, the data of Phase III could be considered as a cross-validation of Phase II, with a larger sample of subjects.

AN ILLUSTRATIVE SAMPLE OF RESULTS

In order to give some idea of the analyses that we performed on the data of Phase II, we will present one three-mode factor analysis, one multivariate analysis of variance, and one table from each of the domains (stereotypes, behavioral intentions, etc.) of the study, and we will list what is available in microfiche in the back of the book.

THREE-MODE ANALYSES

The stereotypes, behavioral intentions, role perceptions, and job perceptions of the samples of Phase II were analyzed by three-mode factor analysis.

In order to illustrate this method as it was used in the present project, we will present one of these analyses. We selected the analysis of role perceptions because it is in some respects the most interesting. Twenty behavioral item scales (shown in Table 1), 104 role pairs (shown in Table 2), and 89 individuals (white female college students, white male high school students, black male high school students, and black male hardcore unemployed) constituted the three modes of the analysis.[1]

---

[1] Two important aspects of this procedure should be mentioned: (1) The variance in cell modes is considered common variance; i.e., no unique or specific factors are specified. (2) All cross-product matrices were found in full; no approximations were used.

Because the three-mode analysis is rather complex, space limitations prevent a complete exposition of the technique here. The reader is referred to Levin (1968) for a clear explanation of the logic of the method and to Tucker (1966) for a technical reference which should allow the interested investigator to perform his own three-mode analysis. Rotation procedures were based on the "raw" Varimax criterion (Harman, 1968) and the Harris-Kaiser (1964) method, which generally results in oblique solutions with respect to the principal components. (This obliqueness is reflected in the "factor intercorrelation matrices" presented in the Results

Table 1 shows what behaviors were seen by the individuals to "go together." The first column shows that *fight with, argue with, hit,* and *threaten* go together. We called this the Hostility dimension. The second column suggests Superordination with Affection (*give orders to, discipline,* and *show affection*). The third column suggests Formal Subordination (*call him Mr., take orders from, work together*). The fourth is Subordination with Affection (*admire, ask permission, love, take orders from,* and *show affection to*). Finally, the last column suggests Friendship (*treat as brother, play games with, relax with,* etc.).[2]

Table 2 shows the roles that have similar content. The first column has large loadings on roles that involve some sort of interracial conflict (e.g., white police–black demonstrator). The second column shows roles that are relatively formal (e.g., teacher-student) and in public situations (at city hall). The third column includes ingroup roles (son, daughter) where the actor has generally lower status than the person acted upon (father, mother). The fourth column includes a wide range of roles being enacted in informal settings (at the park, at a party). The final column includes ingroup roles in which the actor is of generally higher status than the person acted upon (e.g., father-son). We will abbreviate the names of these factors as follows:

1. Interracial Conflict
2. Formal Roles and Situations
3. Ingroup (Low to High Status)
4. Informal Situations
5. Ingroup (High to Low Status)

---

section; actual Pearson r's between the factors, based on subjects' factor scores, are generally much lower.) The final rotation on the core matrix was performed as outlined in Tucker (1966). The cross-products matrix was chosen for the analysis because it allows for mean differences in response magnitude to be reflected in the results of the analyses. These mean differences were of interest to the investigators in interpreting between-groups differences in perception. Table 1 presents the rotated factor matrix of the behavioral items, Table 2 shows the role factors, and Table 3 the core matrix.

[2] This pattern of findings is quite similar to other work which used the role and behavioral differentials. For example, Triandis (1964b) found behavioral intentions which were characterized by five factors. The first (Respect) is similar to factor 4 here, the third (Friendship) resembles factor 5 here, the fourth (Social Distance) reminds us of factor 1, and the fifth (Superordination-Subordination) factor has elements of both the present factors 2 and 3, with reversals in sign where appropriate.

Table 1 Three-Mode Factor Analysis of Behavioral Items

Items	1	2	3	4	5
Admire	−.064	.121	−.075	.479*	−.056
Ask permission of	.108	−.159	.104	.464*	−.080
Fight with	.512*	−.008	−.067	.120	−.056
Love	−.021	.038	−.133	.456*	.033
Take orders from	.117	−.222*	.314*	.353*	−.052
Work together	−.097	.064	.378*	.158	.100
Call him Mr. (her Mrs.)	−.032	−.008	.756*	−.035	.025
Threaten	.389*	.195	.128	−.078	−.046
Discipline	.126	.435*	.224	−.042	−.110
Argue with	.404*	.205	.017	.017	−.051
Laugh together	−.038	.129	.071	.137	.214*
Invite to home	.010	.081	−.157	.179	.275*
Tell personal problems to	.143	−.117	−.121	.189	.266*
Hit	.528*	−.077	−.101	−.049	.143
Treat as a brother	.096	−.173	.128	−.083	.477*
Play games with (cards, pool, etc.)	−.007	.012	.053	−.060	.466*
Relax with	−.043	.062	−.011	−.020	.438*
Invite out to lunch	−.065	.204*	−.022	−.009	.325*
Give orders to	.059	.580*	−.024	−.067	.003
Show affection	−.217*	.425*	−.080	.264*	.036

Note: All loadings rounded to third decimal.
* High loading.
1. Hostility
2. Superordination with Affection
3. Formal Subordination
4. Subordination with Affection
5. Friendship

Table 2 Three-Mode Factor Analysis of Role Pairs

		1	2	3	4	5
Father-son (home)	1	.059	.045	.013	−.056	.267*
Mother-son (home)	2	−.011	.064	.014	.037	.299*
Father-daughter (home)	3	.023	.048	.019	−.047	.288*
Mother-daughter (home)	4	.012	.070	.026	−.050	.278*
Husband-wife (home)	5	.042	.032	.144*	−.063	.179*
Wife-husband (home)	6	.037	.006	.246*	−.061	.088
Son-father (home)	7	−.001	.050	.256*	−.068	.039
Daughter-father (home)	8	.002	.053	.275*	−.055	−.000

Note: All loadings rounded to third decimal.
* High loading.
1. Interracial Conflict
2. Formal Roles and Situations
3. Ingroup (Low to High Status)
4. Informal Situations
5. Ingroup (High to Low Status)

Table 2 (Continued)

		1	2	3	4	5
Son-mother (home)	9	.003	.045	.272*	−.050	.008
Daughter-mother (home)	10	.016	.054	.274*	−.075	.032
Uncle-nephew (home)	11	−.003	.111	.038	−.025	.158*
Cousin-cousin (home)	12	−.014	.061	.123*	.005	.070
Nephew-uncle (home)	13	−.030	.085	.146*	.009	.023
W. foreman–w. worker (work)	14	−.046	.194*	−.074	.023	.109
W. foreman–b. worker (work)	15	.058	.156*	−.048	−.008	.045
B. foreman–w. worker (work)	16	.049	.157*	−.054	.008	.039
B. foreman–b. worker (work)	17	−.021	.218*	−.046	.009	.037
B. cop–w. cop (work)	18	−.014	.184*	.030	.003	−.022
W. cop–b. cop (work)	19	.008	.182*	−.017	.007	.008
W. worker–w. foreman (work)	20	−.045	.166*	.091	.042	−.090
W. worker–b. foreman (work)	21	.055	.111*	.076	.023	−.095
B. worker–w. foreman (work)	22	.064	.111*	.110	.012	−.134*
B. worker–b. foreman (work)	23	−.026	.178*	.102	.020	−.114
B. civil rights leader– b. citizen (work)	24	−.084	.212*	−.004	.007	.087
W. worker–b. worker (work)	25	.082	.115*	−.001	.002	.011
B. worker–w. worker (work)	26	.089	.092	.025	.005	−.007
B. citizen–b. civil rights leader (work)	27	−.054	.200*	−.051	.021	.096
B. teacher–b. student (city hall)	28	.032	.186*	−.087	−.013	.101
B. teacher–w. student (city hall)	29	.083	.137*	−.077	−.012	.091
W. teacher–b. student (city hall)	30	−.027	.181*	−.081	.037	.105
W. teacher–w. student (city hall)	31	.019	.175*	−.039	.009	.048
B. policeman–b. man (city hall)	32	−.020	.192*	−.046	.029	.044
W. policeman–w. man (city hall)	33	−.072	.201*	.086	.041	−.099
B. student–b. teacher (city hall)	34	.069	.138*	.111	−.007	−.130
B. student–w. teacher (city hall)	35	.034	.165*	.077	.017	.136*
W. student–b. teacher (city hall)	36	−.012	.179*	.096	.017	−.105
W. student–w. teacher (city hall)	37	.211*	.046	.029	−.047	−.013
W. revolutionary–b. man (city hall)	38	.054	.125*	.034	.008	−.033
W. civil rights worker–b. man (city hall)	39	−.020	.101*	.075	.057	−.011
W. neighbor–b. neighbor (city hall)	40	.114*	.078	.035	.006	−.025
B. neighbor–w. neighbor (city hall)	41	.063	.142*	.037	−.016	−.024

Note: All loadings rounded to third decimal.
* High loading.
1. Interracial Conflict
2. Formal Roles and Situations
3. Ingroup (Low to High Status)
4. Informal Situations
5. Ingroup (High to Low Status)

Table 2 (Continued)

		1	2	3	4	5
B. man–w. revolutionary (city hall)	42	.179*	.055	.028	−.027	−.026
B. man–w. civil rights leader (city hall)	43	.067	.130*	.044	.003	−.059
W. policeman–b. man (city hall)	44	.146*	.132*	−.067	−.037	.052
W. policeman–b. demonstrator (city hall)	45	.230*	.049	−.058	−.033	.065
B. policeman–w. man (city hall)	46	.060	.140*	−.067	.031	.027
B. man–w. policeman (city hall)	47	.156*	.094	.086	−.032	−.096
B. demonstrator–w. policeman (city hall)	48	.267*	.037	.060	−.071	−.048
W. revolutionary–b. peddler (city hall)	49	.166*	.077	−.011	−.036	.028
B. militant–w. man (city hall)	50	.284*	.029	.002	−.053	−.001
B. civil rights demonstrator–w. segregationist demonstrator (city hall)	51	.257*	.057	.014	−.074	−.003
B. peddler–w. revolutionary (city hall)	52	.145*	.083	.028	−.019	−.036
Father–son (park)	53	.009	−.045	.050	.054	.243*
Mother–son (park)	54	−.005	−.057	.063	.053	.264
Father–daughter (park)	55	−.007	−.058	.055	.081	.221*
Mother–daughter (park)	56	−.014	−.061	.060	.074	.230*
Husband–wife (park)	57	−.014	−.059	.157*	.056	.144*
Wife–husband (park)	58	.005	−.085	.194*	.062	.114
Son–father (park)	59	−.031	−.062	.257*	.085	−.008
Daughter–father (park)	60	.016	−.063	.267*	.040	.011
Son–mother (park)	61	.001	−.076	.241*	.066	.035
Daughter–mother (park)	62	−.018	−.092	.260*	.077	.033
Uncle–nephew (park)	63	−.035	−.042	.023	.121*	.173*
Cousin–cousin (park)	64	−.039	−.007	.064	.111*	.099
Nephew–uncle (park)	65	−.058	−.029	.156*	.125*	.014
W. foreman–w. worker (party)	66	−.057	.027	−.027	.180*	.045
W. foreman–b. worker (party)	67	.012	.026	−.072	.159*	.043
B. foreman–w. worker (party)	68	.004	.008	−.045	.191*	−.003
B. foreman–b. worker (party)	69	−.050	.044	−.035	.176*	.028
B. policeman–w. policeman (party)	70	−.026	.019	−.006	.170*	−.015
W. cop–b. cop (party)	71	.001	.006	−.023	.167*	.024
W. worker–w. foreman (party)	72	−.058	.050	.012	.177*	−.028

Note: All loadings rounded to third decimal.

* High loading.

1. Interracial Conflict
2. Formal Roles and Situations
3. Ingroup (Low to High Status)
4. Informal Situations
5. Ingroup (High to Low Status)

Table 2 (Continued)

		1	2	3	4	5
W. worker–b. foreman (party)	73	.035	− .015	.016	.177*	− .051
B. worker–w. foreman (party)	74	.027	.019	.026	.165*	− .083
B. worker–b. foreman (party)	75	− .088	.058	.044	.175*	− .049
B. civil rights leader–b. citizen (party)	76	− .075	.087	− .023	.162*	.009
W. worker–b. worker (party)	77	.047	− .038	.022	.161	− .025
B. worker–w. worker (party)	78	.028	− .033	.013	.181*	− .027
B. citizen–b. civil rights leader (party)	79	− .057	.048	.055	.149*	− .037
B. teacher–b. student (park)	80	− .086	.106	− .066	.135*	.085
B. teacher–w. student (park)	81	.037	.030	− .064	.134*	.059
W. teacher–b. student (park)	82	.032	− .011	− .069	.161*	.068
W. teacher–w. student (park)	83	− .026	.060	− .047	.127*	.072
B. policeman–b. man (park)	84	− .009	.056	− .074	.145*	.049
W. cop–w. man (park)	85	− .007	.029	− .046	.162*	.034
B. student–b. teacher (park)	86	− .058	.055	.060	.160*	− .070
B. student–w. teacher (park)	87	.025	.015	.041	.163*	− .101
W. student–b. teacher (park)	88	.022	.040	.063	.136*	− .105
W. student–w. teacher (park)	89	− .067	.050	.063	.178*	− .086
W. revolutionary–b. man (park)	90	.167*	− .047	− .009	.093	.011
W. civil rights leader–b. man (park)	91	.071	− .022	− .006	.132*	.011
W. neighbor–b. neighbor (park)	92	.058	− .012	− .014	.145*	.011
B. neighbor–w. neighbor (park)	93	.047	− .025	.007	.145*	− .010
B. man–w. revolutionary (park)	94	.168*	− .066	.010	.112*	− .026
B. man–w. civil rights leader (park)	95	.094	− .031	.008	.145*	− .036
W. cop–b. man (park)	96	.121	− .019	− .062	.107	.060
W. cop–b. demonstrator (park)	97	.241*	− .069	− .071	.059	.095
B. cop–w. man (park)	98	.028	.012	− .062	.179*	.005
B. man–w. policeman (park)	99	.129	− .052	.029	.124*	− .045
B. demonstrator–w. cop (park)	100	.262	− .074	.041	.022	− .018
W. revolutionary–b. peddler (park)	101	.134	− .067	− .016	.127*	.014
B. militant–w. man (park)	102	.252*	− .103*	− .015	.077	.023
B. civil rights demonstrator–w. segregationist demonstrator (park)	103	.253*	− .078	− .042	.073	.037
B. peddler–w. revolutionary (park)	104	.138	− .077	.033	.131*	.040

Note: All loadings rounded to third decimal.
* High loading.
1. Interracial Conflict
2. Formal Roles and Situations
3. Ingroup (Low to High Status)
4. Informal Situations
5. Ingroup (High to Low Status)

Table 3 shows five points of view obtained from our four samples. Table 4 shows the discriminant functions that help us interpret these points of view. The first point of view seems to discriminate the white from the black samples, with the black showing more extreme negative numbers. The second point of view again discriminates blacks and whites, but the signs are reversed. The third suggests that the high school samples have something in common. The fourth suggests that the black high school sample has some unique responses. The fifth again distinguishes blacks and whites.

Table 3 Core Matrix

Sub-ject Fac-tors	Stimulus (Role-Pair) Factors	Behavior Item Factors				
		Hostility	Superordi-nations with Affection	Formal Subordi-nation	Subordi-nations with Affection	Friend-ship
1	1	−234.51	−277.57	−104.50	−249.40	−342.25
	2	−364.29	−360.51	−227.49	−377.25*	−492.24*
	3	−309.49	−292.52	−234.26	−396.48*	−377.20
	4	−386.79*	−409.15*	−211.29	−431.95*	−521.48*
	5	−249.40	−224.84	−186.44	−307.32	−306.34
2	1	14.67	16.21	.68*	19.74	23.00
	2	23.19	22.49	12.36*	24.22*	53.07*
	3	9.26*	2.51*	4.23*	25.24*	25.76*
	4	36.85*	23.15	10.67	25.91*	51.17*
	5	10.36*	−1.29*	−14.68*	22.98	24.40*
3	1	−5.44*	2.22	7.75*	.36	−4.11*
	2	−4.61*	.16	−.43	3.28*	−6.09*
	3	8.66*	2.33	3.72*	−12.98*	4.81*
	4	−1.01	.76	−1.23	.49	−11.85*
	5	.34	2.55*	.75	−16.12*	3.47*
4	1	−11.74*	−12.93*	4.03	−4.25	−2.53
	2	5.22	−10.99*	9.54	−11.63*	−3.94
	3	10.53*	−7.11	2.47	−6.46	−1.63
	4	−2.01	−12.56*	14.78*	−8.84	−9.98
	5	2.51	−3.49	4.42	−10.71*	−3.40
5	1	6.66	4.45	−1.09	2.97	−1.53
	2	8.56*	1.72	2.63	.87	−4.08*
	3	7.65*	−3.82	−2.33	6.44	4.75
	4	2.39	−2.52	1.11	−.26	6.61
	5	1.03	4.16	10.85*	8.82*	−.35

Note: All loadings rounded to second decimal.
* Extreme loading.

Table 4 Discriminant Analysis on Subject-Factor Loadings
(Three-Mode) by Demographic Groups — Role Perceptions

Group Means on Original Factor Loadings

	Factor				
Group	1	2	3	4	5
White female college students	−164.15	26.29	3.65	−1.04	9.02
White high school and Spanish males	−164.12	29.11	−1.87	−2.03	1.12
Black high school males	−193.97	−4.82	−2.51	6.36	−6.62
Black hardcore males	−190.97	−29.87	1.15	−3.89	−.21

Scaled Vectors of Discriminant Functions

Factors	Function 1	Function 2
1	81.36	−97.92
2	193.66	75.24
3	5.00	−47.58
4	5.35	88.63
5	66.14	−104.08
% of variance	88.32	10.35

Group Means on Discriminant Functions

Group	Function 1	Function 2
White female college students	−34.71	74.05
White high school and Spanish males	−35.76	80.77
Black high school males	−77.95	92.20
Black hardcore males	−95.30	72.88

Overall F ratio $= 6.37$ $(df = 15,224)$, $p < .01$.

The discriminant functions tell us that the four samples differ in two major ways. One is a contrast of blacks and whites which depends primarily on the second point of view but also on the first and fifth. The other is a contrast between the high school boys and the others, which involves a contrast of the first, third, and fifth points of view on the one hand with the second and fourth points of view on the other hand.

Examination of the mean responses of the four samples to a wide range of roles suggests that all samples show low Hostility, low Superordination with Affection, low Formal Subordination, low Subordination with Affection, and low Friendship. The blacks of the first point of view show this pattern in a stronger manner than do the whites. We can interpret this pattern as suggestive of "caution" in role relationships, but it could also be due to a lack of clarity in the roles. The fact that all samples give judgments around 2, 3, or 4 rather than 7, 8, or 9 on a 10-point scale would suggest they do not feel confident about their judgments. The blacks are even more likely than the whites to use a 2, 3, or 4 rather than larger numbers.

The second point of view contrasts the majority whites, who show some Hostility, Superordination with Affection, Formal Subordination, Subordination with Affection, and Friendship in Formal Roles and Situations and Informal Situations, with the blacks. Blacks tended to react to these situations with caution or with lack of clarity concerning what is appropriate behavior. The blacks of this viewpoint show greater Formal Subordination (*call him Mr., Mrs.,* etc.) in all roles and situations when compared to the whites; they also show more Hostility and more Superordination with Affection in Ingroup roles.

The third point of view contrasts the high school boys, both black and white, with the other samples. It reflects high Subordination with Affection in Ingroup roles, high Friendship in Informal Situations as well as in Formal Roles and Situations, and high Hostility in Interracial Conflict situations and in Formal Roles and Situations.

The fourth point of view contrasts the black high school boys with the other sample. This sample is unusually high relative to the other samples in perceiving Hostility in Interracial Conflict roles, Subordination with Affection in Formal Roles and Ingroup (High to Low Status) roles, and Superordination with Affection in Interracial Conflict roles, Formal Roles and Situations, and Informal Situations. They also see unusually little Hostility in Ingroup (Low to High Status) roles.

The fifth point of view contrasts a minority viewpoint of blacks who show very high Formal Subordination and high Subordination with Affection in Ingroup (High-Low Status) roles and much Hostility in Formal Roles and Situations and Ingroup (Low-High Status) roles. The whites of this point of view see little Friendship in Formal Roles and Situations.

We interpret these findings as showing that the majority white versus majority black points of view (viewpoints 1 and 2) are different in that the white response pattern suggests more certainty about roles and involves greater willingness to express Hostility and Friendship, while the black allows Hostility to occur only in Ingroup roles (where presumably the whites will not punish the behavior) and shows a more authoritarian pattern of behavior in Ingroup roles (more superordination, but also more acceptance of the ingroup). Finally, the blacks show much Formal Subordination (*call him Mr.,* etc.), which suggests a greater need for the exchange of status in intimate relationships. One could speculate that lack of resources in the black ghetto lead to more cautious relationships. Furthermore, the deprivation of status which is created by white society leads to a greater need for the exchange of status.

The minority black and white points of view, reflected in viewpoint 5, show blacks who are "at ease" in most human relationships and whites who show less Friendship in Formal Roles and Situations. "At ease" is here interpreted as a situation where Hostility can be expressed in Formal Roles and Situations as well as in Ingroup (Low-High Status) situations.

The high school boys of both races seem to share the characteristics of high Subordination with Affection in Ingroup roles and high Friendship in many situations but also much Hostility in Interracial Conflict situations and Formal Roles and Situations. This might be interpreted as a situation of great polarization of interracial conflict in high schools in the early 1970s.

The black high school boys are characterized by unusually high perceived Interracial Conflict. They also seem to have unusually suppressed perceived Hostility in the Ingroup (Low-High Status) roles (e.g., son-father).

Similar analyses are available for the other domains. In microfiche, the numbers for the tables are shown as MF 1, MF 2, etc. Thus the three-mode factor analysis of the stereotypes is presented on MF 1 to MF 4. The corresponding analyses of the behavioral intentions are on MF 31 to MF 34, the job perceptions on MF 93 to MF 97.

PHASE III

The most interesting findings of Phase II were used to select the questions utilized in Phase III. The latter phase was based on a systematic sample, with 10 subjects in each of the 24 cells of a $2 \times 2 \times 2 \times 3$ design, in which we varied systematically the race, age, sex, and social class of the subjects.

A multivariate analysis of variance was used to determine the way the independent variables (race, sex, age, and social class) relate to the dependent variables (stereotypes, behavioral intentions, role perceptions, job perceptions). In addition, the implicative relationships were analyzed by an approach which maximally discriminates the four samples of Phase II, and the implicative relationships of Phase III were again analyzed through multivariate analysis of variance.

In order to provide some impressions of the kinds of data and analyses we have done for each of the domains, we will present one or two tables from each domain.

Stereotypes. Table 5 presents the stereotypes of WHITE WOMEN obtained from the 24 samples of Phase III. Each cell is the average of the responses of 10 subjects judging this stimulus on scales such as *trustworthy, hard-working,* etc. Each scale varied from 0 (never has this characteristic) to 9 (always has this characteristic). The footnotes indicate which of the effects were significant, on the basis of the multivariate analysis of variance. It is shown, for instance, that blacks, when compared with whites, tend to see WHITE WOMEN as low on the scales *trustworthy, lazy,* and *important* and high on *aggressive* and *active.* The midpoint of all scales is 4.5. Note that all white samples judge the stimulus above the midpoint on *trustworthy,* but two black samples deviate from this pattern and judge it to be untrustworthy.

Behavioral intentions. Table 6 continues the illustration with behavioral intentions toward WHITE WOMEN. We note several significant effects in the attached footnotes. Whites are more likely to *help, go out with, trust,* and *respect,* and blacks more likely to *stay away from,* this stimulus.

Role perceptions. Table 7 illustrates the analysis of role perceptions. The analysis suggests a more positive relationship between mother and daughter among blacks than among whites.

Job perceptions. To illustrate the way SECRETARIES are perceived by the samples of Phase III, we present Table 8. Apparently there is no reliable race effect, but there are strong effects for social class and sex. The hardcore and the working class seem to have a very positive image of this job, while the middle class see it less positively; females have a more positive view of this job than do males. These findings, of course, are in no way startling. They simply indicate that our procedures result in data that can be trusted. When we obtain data that are unexpected, we can pay attention to them precisely because the majority of the obtained data are reasonable. It is in the *context* of similarities across samples that differences "make sense."

Implicative relations. Here we examine the perceived antecedents and consequents of important events, such as TO FINISH COLLEGE. Table 9 shows the three clusters of responses to the antecedents of TO FINISH COLLEGE. We see that one dimension involves the idea of working hard (*be willing to work, study hard, do the work teachers assign*), the idea of being confident (*believe in yourself*), and the idea of being motivated (*go to classes, know what you want, be interested, have right attitude, want to learn*). The second dimension considers the factors of drive and social pressure (*have friends in college*). The third dimension considers economic capability and incentives as well as ability factors.

Table 10 shows the means of the four samples of Phase II on these three dimensions. We note the tendency of the black hardcore (sample 4) to be low on the first dimension (in short, they do not consider hard work, confidence, and motivation as important as do the other groups). The black high school students are low on the second dimension; i.e., they do not consider drive and social pressures as important as do the other samples. The white high school students are particularly likely to be high on the third dimension; they consider financial incentives and capability particularly important.

Two discriminant functions distinguish the four groups in a dependable ($p < .01$) manner. The first is a reflection of the first dimension and separates the hardcore blacks from the other samples (bottom of Table 9), while the second discriminant function reflects mostly the third dimension and separates the high school white students from the other samples. In short, this analysis tells us that the black hardcore and the white high school students are the two groups that differ from the other groups, the former being different on the first dimension and the latter being different on the third dimension.

We conclude, then, that the hardcore blacks see less hard work, motivation, and self-confidence as necessary for graduation from college than do the other groups; the white high school students see more financial capability and incentive as necessary.

Table 5 Stereotypes of WHITE WOMEN

	Independent Variables		Trust-worthy	Hard-working	Intelli-gent	Active	Lazy	Unim-portant	Tough	Aggres-sive
BLACKS	Hardcore	Female 18–25	5.0	5.3	5.2	5.0	3.0	4.2	4.0	5.4
		35–45	5.0	5.4	5.1	5.5	3.9	2.7	3.1	6.6
		Male 18–25	5.2	4.9	4.7	5.2	3.5	3.0	2.9	4.5
		35–45	4.4	5.7	5.5	5.5	2.3	2.2	3.2	5.3
	Working Class	Female 18–25	4.6	5.1	4.6	5.7	3.7	3.1	1.8	4.0
		35–45	4.6	5.2	5.3	5.4	3.1	1.5	3.0	5.8
		Male 18–25	4.9	4.5	5.4	5.6	3.3	2.7	3.3	5.6
		35–45	4.9	6.2	6.2	6.6	2.3	1.7	2.9	6.7
	Middle Class	Female 18–25	4.7	4.5	4.5	5.2	3.1	1.7	3.4	5.1
		35–45	4.5	4.9	5.0	5.1	3.1	2.2	3.3	5.9
		Male 18–25	4.2	5.0	5.3	5.6	2.8	2.5	2.5	4.3
		35–45	5.5	5.7	5.5	5.9	3.3	2.6	3.5	5.1

WHITES										
Hardcore	Female	18-25	4.7	5.3	5.0	4.7	4.0	1.4	3.3	4.6
		35-45	5.5	5.1	4.7	4.3	2.7	.7	2.6	3.2
	Male	18-25	5.1	5.3	5.4	5.4	3.9	2.1	3.6	5.2
		35-45	4.9	6.0	5.6	6.3	3.6	2.0	4.4	4.4
Working Class	Female	18-25	6.0	6.2	5.7	6.0	3.1	1.1	3.8	4.4
		35-45	5.2	5.8	5.1	5.8	3.8	1.4	2.8	4.2
	Male	18-25	5.1	4.9	4.8	5.4	3.9	1.9	4.1	5.0
		35-45	5.6	5.2	5.7	5.7	3.9	2.4	2.9	4.4
Middle Class	Female	18-25	5.6	5.6	5.4	4.9	3.9	1.0	4.0	4.1
		35-45	4.9	4.7	4.7	4.2	4.0	1.7	3.7	3.9
	Male	18-25	5.5	5.2	5.6	5.2	4.3	2.9	2.7	4.6
		35-45	5.6	5.4	5.6	5.5	3.9	2.4	3.8	4.3

1. Main effect for race ($p < .0001$): Univariate tests indicate that blacks see WHITE WOMEN as less *trustworthy*, less *lazy*, less *important*, and more *aggressive* than whites do, while the multivariate tests indicate that the effects are due to specific variance. The multivariate tests also indicate that for the variance specific to the active variable, blacks see WHITE WOMEN as more active than whites see them.

2. Race × age interaction ($p < .05$): Univariate and multivariate F tests indicate that young blacks see WHITE WOMEN as more *aggressive* than older blacks, while young whites see WHITE WOMEN as less *aggressive* than older whites.

Table 6 Behavioral Intentions Toward WHITE WOMEN

	Independent Variables		Help	Go Out with	Trust	Respect	Criticize	Stay Away from	Ask for Advice
	Female	18–25	3.7	1.6	3.3	3.9	4.4	3.7	2.2
		35–45	3.8	2.0	3.8	5.0	2.8	3.7	2.8
Hardcore	Male	18–25	4.9	4.0	2.8	4.7	3.0	3.9	3.0
		35–45	4.0	2.6	3.7	5.7	2.5	4.0	3.0
	Female	18–25	3.8	2.0	3.5	5.4	4.0	3.1	1.5
		35–45	4.6	2.3	4.5	5.4	4.1	4.3	2.8
BLACKS Working Class	Male	18–25	3.9	2.2	2.7	4.1	4.0	5.1	2.4
		35–45	4.8	2.4	5.3	7.0	2.8	3.9	2.2
	Female	18–25	4.3	3.1	3.5	4.4	3.8	3.6	2.6
		35–45	4.0	3.3	3.0	4.4	3.8	3.6	2.3
Middle Class	Male	18–25	4.7	3.3	4.7	5.8	3.7	3.8	2.2
		35–45	4.9	3.7	5.0	5.9	3.5	4.3	2.3
	Female	18–25	6.7	5.4	5.7	5.9	3.6	2.4	3.6
		35–45	5.0	3.8	4.6	5.2	4.1	2.2	2.9
Hardcore	Male	18–25	4.5	5.9	4.6	5.5	2.8	2.9	1.9
		35–45	6.6	6.2	4.4	5.9	2.8	2.5	3.3

WHITES Working Class	Female	18–25	6.7	2.9	6.2	6.3	3.4	2.3	6.2
		35–45	5.9	4.2	5.3	5.6	4.6	3.0	3.1
	Male	18–25	6.5	7.3	4.3	5.4	4.3	2.3	2.4
		35–45	5.3	6.9	5.5	5.9	3.7	1.6	2.0
Middle Class	Female	18–25	6.3	6.6	6.0	6.0	3.8	2.2	5.1
		35–45	5.7	6.6	6.1	6.0	3.7	1.4	4.1
	Male	18–25	6.3	7.2	6.0	5.9	4.5	1.5	4.8
		35–45	6.4	6.1	6.2	6.4	4.6	1.7	3.7

1. Contrast for blacks versus whites ($p < .0000$): Whites are more likely to *help*, *go out with*, *trust*, and *respect* WHITE WOMEN; blacks are more likely to *stay away from*, according to univariate and multivariate tests. Univariate tests indicate *ask for advice* shares common variance with *help* and *go out with*.

2. Contrast for socioeconomic status ($p < .0090$): Middle-class persons are most likely to *go out with* and *trust* WHITE WOMEN; working-class are least likely to *go out with* and hardcore are least likely to *trust* them, according to univariate and multivariate tests.

3. Contrast for sex ($p < .0001$): Males are most likely to *go out with* WHITE WOMEN as shown in univariate and multivariate tests. Multivariate tests show variance unique to *ask for advice*, with females more likely to ask white women for advice.

4. Contrast for race × sex ($p < .0097$): As indicated by both univariate and multivariate analyses, the patterns for *trust* and *ask for advice* are the same; white females are most likely to do these, followed by white males, black males, and black females. Multivariate tests show variance unique to *go out with* following the same pattern except that white males are most likely to *go out with* WHITE WOMEN and white females are second most likely.

5. Contrast for socioeconomic status × sex ($p < .0115$): Middle-class males are most likely to *trust* WHITE WOMEN, more so than middle-class females. However, in the other two classes, females are more likely to *trust* WHITE WOMEN. This is shown in both univariate and multivariate tests. Variance unique to *go out with* shows middle-class males most likely to *go out with* WHITE WOMEN, and males in the working class and hardcore classes next most likely. Working-class females are the least likely, according to multivariate tests.

Table 7 Role-Pair Perceptions of Mother-Daughter (at home)

Independent Variables			Work To-gether	Fight with	Treat as a Brother	Call Him Mr.	Love	Ad-mire	Play Games with	Disci-pline	Hit	Give Orders to
BLACKS	Hardcore	Female	18–25	6.5	2.4	3.3	2.9	7.3	7.2	5.2	5.1	2.7	4.8
			35–45	5.6	1.8	2.7	.6	7.5	7.7	3.8	5.4	2.4	5.4
		Male	18–25	6.1	2.7	3.9	1.1	7.8	7.1	5.9	6.5	2.7	5.2
			35–45	6.2	.9	4.1	2.6	7.4	6.5	3.9	6.6	1.9	5.4
	Working Class	Female	18–25	6.3	2.8	2.0	2.6	7.7	7.5	5.1	6.6	3.5	6.5
			35–45	7.0	.9	2.8	.8	8.7	7.3	4.6	5.0	1.3	6.2
		Male	18–25	7.0	2.0	3.7	1.7	8.7	8.1	5.4	6.0	2.5	5.7
			35–45	5.5	2.1	2.9	1.2	6.9	6.5	4.6	5.8	1.9	5.8
	Middle Class	Female	18–25	6.1	2.0	1.7	.7	8.1	6.8	4.9	6.8	2.8	7.4
			35–45	6.8	2.1	3.0	1.1	8.3	8.2	5.5	6.1	1.7	5.2
		Male	18–25	6.0	2.3	2.9	1.1	7.9	7.6	5.3	7.0	2.0	6.9
			35–45	6.3	1.6	4.0	.7	7.7	7.2	5.4	5.9	2.6	6.7

WHITES	Hardcore	Female	18–25	5.4	3.7	2.6	.6	7.8	6.2	4.7	7.0	2.7	6.5
			35–45	6.6	2.0	2.0	.5	7.6	6.6	4.8	6.8	2.7	7.2
		Male	18–25	6.3	2.1	2.5	2.0	7.6	6.7	5.3	5.4	2.5	5.6
			35–45	7.2	2.6	2.0	2.7	7.5	6.5	5.8	4.9	1.5	4.3
	Working Class	Female	18–25	6.5	3.1	1.9	.5	7.7	5.6	4.9	6.7	2.1	6.5
			35–45	5.4	2.8	1.2	1.4	8.5	7.3	4.5	6.4	2.2	5.4
		Male	18–25	5.1	3.5	.3	.3	7.4	5.5	4.3	5.6	3.1	4.5
			35–45	5.2	2.9	3.2	1.5	7.4	6.8	5.5	5.5	2.4	5.8
	Middle Class	Female	18–25	6.6	3.1	4.0	.6	7.1	5.9	5.9	5.5	2.4	6.6
			35–45	5.6	3.6	1.4	.5	7.3	6.6	5.1	6.0	2.8	5.0
		Male	18–25	5.9	4.3	1.9	.6	6.7	5.1	4.3	6.0	3.4	6.9
			35–45	6.2	2.8	4.5	.6	7.8	6.9	4.8	6.8	1.9	5.7

1. Main effect for race ($p < .0001$): Univariate and multivariate tests indicate blacks see a mother as less likely to *fight with* her daughter, more likely to *admire* and *treat as a brother*, than whites do.

Table 8 Job Perceptions of SECRETARIES

Independent Variables			Lazy	Well Paid	Travel a Lot	Good Future	Polite	Skilled	Under-standing	Dirty
	Female	18–25	2.5	6.6	3.8	6.8	6.6	7.7	6.2	1.0
		35–45	2.6	5.0	2.7	4.7	6.0	6.2	4.9	1.0
Hardcore	Male	18–25	3.4	5.0	3.0	4.6	6.5	5.7	5.5	1.7
		35–45	1.9	11.1	3.5	5.9	7.4	7.4	7.4	.8
	Female	18–25	1.9	5.3	2.8	6.6	5.9	7.7	6.1	.5
		35–45	3.0	5.1	2.9	7.0	6.4	7.2	6.2	.8
BLACKS Working Class	Male	18–25	3.8	5.3	3.1	5.4	6.0	6.7	4.8	1.6
		35–45	2.3	4.6	2.7	5.1	5.6	6.7	5.4	1.8
	Female	18–25	3.4	3.3	2.1	3.5	5.0	6.1	4.5	1.6
		35–45	2.4	4.5	3.1	4.9	6.3	6.8	5.1	1.2
Middle Class	Male	18–25	2.4	3.3	2.8	4.0	5.7	6.2	4.6	.8
		35–45	1.9	4.0	2.3	4.1	6.7	6.4	5.9	1.5
	Female	18–25	1.9	5.4	2.5	5.5	6.4	6.7	5.1	.8
		35–45	1.7	5.3	3.2	5.5	6.6	7.3	6.3	1.2
Hardcore	Male	18–25	2.3	4.8	3.0	4.4	6.9	7.3	5.7	1.7
		35–45	2.5	3.5	3.2	3.5	5.8	6.1	4.5	1.8

WHITES Working Class	Female	18–25	1.5	5.3	2.8	6.4	7.7	8.4	5.9	.8
		35–45	2.6	5.4	3.0	4.5	6.2	7.5	5.4	1.2
	Male	18–25	2.8	3.8	2.5	4.0	4.9	5.7	4.4	2.0
		35–45	2.9	4.3	2.3	5.0	6.0	5.9	5.3	2.0
Middle Class	Female	18–25	2.6	2.9	2.1	4.3	6.7	6.7	5.0	1.8
		35–45	3.1	4.3	2.6	4.0	6.0	6.1	4.2	1.3
	Male	18–25	3.4	3.4	3.1	3.8	6.0	5.2	5.0	1.5
		35–45	3.4	4.8	3.1	4.5	6.8	6.7	5.7	2.0

1. Contrast for race ($p < .0633$): Univariate and multivariate tests both indicate that blacks are more likely than whites to see SECRETARIES as having a good future.

2. Contrast for socioeconomic class ($p < .0001$): Univariate and multivariate tests show that the hardcore is most likely to think SECRETARIES are well paid, while the middle class is least likely to think so. The working class is most likely to see SECRETARIES as having a good future, the middle class is least likely to think so. Univariate tests show the working class most likely to see SECRETARIES as skilled, the middle class least likely. This item appears to share common variance with good future.

3. Contrast for sex ($p < .0005$): Univariate and multivariate tests indicate that females are more likely than males to see SECRETARIES as having a good future and as being skilled. Univariate tests show males are more likely to see SECRETARIES as having a dirty job, though this appears inversely related to skilled.

4. Contrast for race × socioeconomic status × sex × age ($p < .0381$): Univariate and multivariate tests show that the older, working-class, black females are most likely to see SECRETARIES as having a good future. In general, females, blacks, working-class and older people are most likely to see SECRETARIES as having a good future. Univariate tests show nice, skilled, and understanding as being related and sharing variance with good future.

Table 9 Antecedents of TO FINISH COLLEGE

Items	Rotated Factor Matrix		
	1	2	3
Be willing to work	1.58*	.25	.11
Have drive	.98	1.58*	−.84
Go to classes	2.00*	−.27	.08
Study hard	2.05*	−.16	−.13
Know what you want to do	1.48*	.43	−.15
Have friends in college	−.62	1.97*	.39
Be interested in (dig) what you are doing	1.45*	.46	−.06
Have the right attitude	1.69*	.05	.11
Do the work the teachers assign	1.96*	−.61	.39
Be smart	.30	.62	1.35*
Have money	−.11	−.13	2.11*
Want to "live good"	.10	.57	1.25*
Want to learn	2.16*	−.38	−.03
Believe in yourself	1.87*	.29	−.40
Get along with the teachers	.96	.10	.90

1. Work and confidence
2. Ambition — social pressure
3. Financial incentive — capability

Factor Correlation Matrix

	1	2
1		
2	0.95	
3	0.95	0.93

* Highest factor loading.

Group Means on Original Factor Scores

Group	1	2	3
1	3.92	3.39	2.96
2	3.67	3.29	3.61
3	4.30	2.22	3.37
4	3.23	3.06	2.84

Discriminant Functions

Factors	Function 1	Function 2
1	.9164	−.4170
2	−.3632	−.0151
3	.1683	−.9088
4		
5		
6		
% of variance	71.3	26.5

Table 9 (Continued)

Group Means on Discriminant Functions

Group	Function 1	Function 2
1	2.86	−1.11
2	2.77	−1.80
3	3.34	−1.32
4	2.33	−1.28

Overall F ratio 3.18 ($df = 9{,}226$), $p < .01$.

In Table 10 we have the consequents of TO FINISH COLLEGE. Three clusters of consequents are shown in the first part of the table: (a) accomplishment — *get good job, get better pay, feel accomplishment, get respect from others, plan future, move into own apartment, believe in yourself;* (b) independence — *get married, don't have to depend on others;* and (c) future obligations — *get more education, go into military service.*

Three dimensions discriminate the four groups of Phase II in a dependable manner (see the last part of the table). The first seems to set apart the girls from the boys and the hardcore. This is natural since this dimension reflects the factor of future obligations and the girls do not have military obligations. Consistently, the two high school samples are the highest on this discriminant function because they are the most likely to go into the military (the data were collected in 1970).

The second discriminant function distinguishes the hardcore blacks from the other samples. It reflects mostly the responses to the first factor, on which they are low. This means that the hardcore blacks see less accomplishment as a consequent of TO FINISH COLLEGE than do the other samples.

Finally, the third dimension distinguishes the white high school students from the other samples and depends on responses to both the second and the third factors — i.e., they are relatively high on "independence" and on "future obligations."

The black hardcore are different from the other samples in that they see less motivation and hard work as necessary TO FINISH COLLEGE and less accomplishment as a consequence of this event. In short, they devalue the event. This is a "sour grapes" effect which one might have expected. The white high school students see independence following this event, but the black samples do not stress independence so much. This is probably a reflection of the fact that the blacks already have a good deal of independence and do not see it connected with college graduation. We conclude that these data support the concept that people will evaluate less highly those desirable events to which they do not have access.

Table 10   Consequents of TO FINISH COLLEGE

Items	Rotated Factor Matrix		
	1	2	3
Get a good job	1.89*	−.25	.49
Work harder	1.41*	.18	.35
Get better pay	2.21*	.29	−.47
Feel important	1.31*	.83	−.14
Get married	.03	2.05*	−.12
Don't have to depend on others	−.24	1.82*	.42
Have some of the "finer things in life" ("live good")	1.06*	.53	.58
Get more education (law school, medical school)	1.32*	−.58	1.53*
Go into military service (Army, Navy, etc.)	−.45	.22	2.42*
Feel that you've accomplished something	2.18*	−.53	.40
Get respect from other people	2.08*	−.02	−.20
Plan for the future	2.33*	−.17	−.18
Move into your own apartment	2.17*	.13	−.41
Have your parents treat you better	1.38*	.44	.10
Believe in yourself	2.46*	−.05	−.38

1. Accomplishment
2. Independence
3. Future obligations

Factor Correlation Matrix

	1	2
1		
2	0.94	
3	0.92	0.91

* Highest factor loading.

Group Means on Original Factor Scores

Group	1	2	3
1	3.57	3.39	2.13
2	3.32	3.22	2.96
3	3.48	2.72	2.68
4	3.06	2.92	2.31

Table 10 (Continued)

Discriminant Functions

Factors	Function 1	Function 2	Function 3
1	.3069	−.9865	.3518
2	−.5710	−.1387	−.7634
3	.7614	.0876	−.5417
4			
5			
6			
% of variance	49.7	32.5	17.8

Group Means on Discriminant Functions

Group	Function 1	Function 2	Function 3
1	.78	−3.80	−2.49
2	1.43	−3.47	−2.89
3	1.56	−3.58	−2.30
4	1.03	−3.22	−2.40

Overall F ratio 2.94 ($df = 9,222$), $p < .01$.

To illustrate the analysis of implicative relationships obtained with data of Phase III, we present Tables 11 and 12. These tables are similar in interpretation to the other tables we have presented from that phase.

The Appendix lists the 128 tables presented in microfiche. Interested readers will find a good deal of information in these tables.

Table 11 Antecedents of TO FINISH HIGH SCHOOL

	Independent Variables		Do Work Given	Want to Go to College	Be Interested in School Work	Come to School Each Day	Please Teachers	Passing Grades	Be Smart
BLACKS									
	Hardcore	Female							
		18–25	7.7	2.8	5.0	8.2	5.4	7.3	5.3
		35–45	8.2	2.4	8.1	8.4	5.3	8.4	6.0
		Male							
		18–25	7.4	2.5	6.9	7.1	4.3	7.1	7.1
		35–45	8.6	5.0	8.7	8.2	6.4	8.0	7.1
	Working Class	Female							
		18–25	8.1	2.0	7.2	7.3	4.0	8.7	4.4
		35–45	7.3	3.9	7.3	8.2	4.4	8.5	5.8
		Male							
		18–25	8.0	4.0	7.0	7.4	3.4	8.5	5.8
		35–45	7.7	3.9	8.2	8.2	5.9	8.6	6.8
	Middle Class	Female							
		18–25	7.8	1.5	6.5	7.1	3.8	7.9	4.5
		35–45	7.4	2.1	5.7	6.6	3.8	8.4	3.6
		Male							
		18–25	6.3	2.2	3.5	5.0	3.9	7.7	3.6
		35–45	7.5	3.5	7.0	7.4	4.0	8.0	5.9

			7.4	1.4	5.7	5.8	5.1	8.5	4.2	
	Female	18–25	8.9	3.4	7.9	8.1	5.4	8.0	6.4	
		35–45								
Hardcore										
			8.3	2.2	6.2	7.5	3.5	8.6	6.0	
	Male	18–25	7.9	5.4	7.6	7.8	4.8	7.5	5.7	
		35–45								
			7.2	3.1	5.8	7.0	3.9	8.3	5.1	
	Female	18–25	8.0	2.7	6.8	6.7	4.7	7.6	5.3	
		35–45								
WHITES Working Class										
			7.7	1.9	4.7	6.7	4.2	8.5	4.6	
	Male	18–25	8.3	2.4	6.2	7.0	3.1	8.2	4.7	
		35–45								
			6.8	1.7	3.5	4.8	3.9	8.2	2.9	
	Female	18–25	7.1	1.5	5.5	6.6	3.2	8.3	4.1	
		35–45								
Middle Class										
			6.6	3.3	3.6	5.0	3.8	7.9	3.8	
	Male	18–25	7.4	3.8	6.1	6.7	4.9	8.4	5.1	
		35–45								

Table 11 (Continued)

Independent Variables				Stay Out of Trouble	Want to Finish	Want to Learn	Ask for Help	Study Hard	Get Along with Teachers	Want Good Job	Have Friends– Drop-outs
BLACKS	Working Class	Hardcore	Female 18–25	6.5	6.6	7.2	7.6	7.6	6.3	5.6	2.8
			35–45	6.8	7.9	8.1	8.3	7.9	7.4	6.6	1.1
			Male 18–25	6.4	7.8	7.5	6.6	6.6	6.1	6.0	2.9
			35–45	7.8	8.8	8.5	8.4	8.3	8.5	7.0	2.0
			Female 18–25	6.0	8.5	6.8	7.1	6.5	6.3	4.3	.9
			35–45	6.8	8.3	7.9	8.7	7.8	6.5	6.5	1.4
			Male 18–25	6.4	8.0	7.5	7.3	7.3	6.4	7.0	2.4
			35–45	7.4	8.5	8.3	8.3	8.3	7.6	7.8	.5
	Middle Class		Female 18–25	5.1	7.6	7.1	7.3	6.6	5.3	4.2	1.3
			35–45	6.2	7.8	6.4	5.7	5.6	5.5	4.1	1.3
			Male 18–25	4.6	6.2	4.8	4.9	3.9	5.1	3.8	1.2
			35–45	6.3	7.9	7.5	7.5	7.6	6.9	5.3	1.5
		Hardcore	Female 18–25	4.8	7.2	5.8	6.5	5.4	4.8	3.8	.9
			35–45	7.0	8.1	7.5	7.6	7.3	7.3	7.5	1.6
			Male 18–25	7.2	8.2	7.4	7.2	7.0	6.8	5.3	1.6
			35–45	6.4	8.0	7.7	7.2	7.3	7.0	6.7	2.5

WHITES										
Working Class	Female	18–25	6.3	7.1	6.3	6.1	6.4	5.3	5.4	1.4
		35–45	6.5	8.2	7.8	7.3	7.5	6.3	7.7	1.7
	Male	18–25	6.0	7.7	6.6	6.7	5.2	5.7	5.6	1.3
		35–45	6.6	7.4	7.3	6.4	6.5	5.5	5.6	1.2
Middle Class	Female	18–25	5.2	6.9	4.1	3.9	3.9	4.6	4.2	.7
		35–45	5.8	7.3	6.4	5.9	5.1	5.7	3.8	1.3
	Male	18–25	5.1	6.4	3.9	3.9	3.7	4.2	3.9	1.4
		35–45	5.7	8.2	6.2	4.7	5.0	5.4	5.1	1.9

1. Main effect for race ($p < .0001$): According to both multivariate and univariate tests, blacks are more likely than whites to see *be interested in school work, come to school each day, want to learn,* and *ask for help* as being necessary TO FINISH HIGH SCHOOL. Multivariate tests indicate a variance unique to *passing grades* that shows whites are more likely to see this as necessary TO FINISH HIGH SCHOOL. Univariate tests show blacks as most likely to see *be smart, study hard,* and *get along with teachers* as necessary TO FINISH HIGH SCHOOL, but these items share common variance with others.

2. Main effect for socioeconomic status ($p < .0001$): Univariate and multivariate tests show that the hardcore is the most likely to see as necessary TO FINISH HIGH SCHOOL: *do work given, be interested in school work, come to school each day, be smart,* and *ask for help.* The working class is close behind, but the middle class is a distant third in viewing these things as necessities. Multivariate tests indicate that the variance unique to *passing grades* shows that the middle class is most likely to see this as helping TO FINISH HIGH SCHOOL, whereas the working class is least likely to view *passing grades* in this way.

3. Main effect for sex ($p < .0323$): Males are more likely to see *want to go to college* and *be smart* as necessary for finishing high school according to both univariate and multivariate tests. Multivariate tests show that the variance unique to *ask for help* shows females as more likely than males to see this as a prerequisite for finishing high school.

4. Main effect for age ($p < .0001$): Older people are more likely than younger people to view *do work given, want to go to college,* and *be interested in school work* as necessary for a person TO FINISH HIGH SCHOOL. Variance unique to getting *passing grades* shows older people are slightly more likely to see this as a factor in getting out of high school. Univariate tests show *come to school each day* related to *be interested in school work. Be smart, stay out of trouble, want to finish, want to learn, ask for help, study hard, get along with teachers,* and *want good job* are all interrelated and share variance.

Table 12 Consequents of TO FINISH HIGH SCHOOL

	Independent Variables		Get a Job	Go into the Military	Go to College	Buy a Car	Feel Proud of Yourself	Start to Plan Future	Get Married	Feel More Mature
		Female	18–25	5.4	2.5	3.4	2.7	7.1	6.6	2.8	6.9
			35–45	6.2	3.2	4.9	3.3	8.0	7.3	3.5	6.5
	Hardcore	Male	18–25	6.2	4.9	6.2	3.8	8.1	7.1	3.5	7.0
			35–45	5.7	4.0	3.6	3.0	6.5	6.1	3.3	6.8
		Female	18–25	6.0	4.0	4.6	2.9	7.7	6.6	4.3	6.5
			35–45	6.4	3.8	4.9	3.8	7.8	7.1	4.1	6.4
BLACKS	Working Class	Male	18–25	6.5	5.3	4.7	3.9	7.3	6.8	3.5	7.6
			35–45	5.3	4.6	3.6	2.9	6.9	6.5	3.1	6.6
		Female	18–25	4.2	3.3	4.9	3.3	7.2	7.2	4.3	6.1
			35–45	4.9	3.9	5.1	2.6	7.6	6.7	3.4	5.6
	Middle Class	Male	18–25	6.2	3.8	6.4	4.4	6.9	6.4	2.6	7.1
			35–45	6.4	4.2	5.0	2.5	6.7	6.2	3.8	4.8
		Female	18–25	6.0	4.7	5.2	3.4	6.8	6.9	4.0	6.0
			35–45	5.7	3.0	4.6	3.4	7.1	7.2	3.5	6.6
	Hardcore	Male	18–25	4.9	2.8	4.3	4.5	6.9	6.6	3.2	6.0
			35–45	6.7	4.3	6.1	4.5	6.7	7.1	4.6	7.1

	Independent Variables		Get Respect	Don't Depend on Others	Lazy for a While	Glad Not to Listen to Teachers	Get Job Training	Move into Own Apartment	Treated Better by Parents
WHITES	Working Class	Female 18–25	6.4	3.0	3.4	7.5	8.1	3.6	6.4
		35–45	6.3	4.2	3.2	6.7	6.3	3.1	6.1
		Male 18–25	5.8	3.7	5.5	6.7	6.6	2.9	5.7
		35–45	6.5	4.5	3.8	6.2	6.0	3.7	6.3
	Middle Class	Female 18–25	6.3	3.9	3.3	5.2	6.1	4.0	6.6
		35–45	5.6	3.3	2.7	6.9	6.7	2.9	6.2
		Male 18–25	5.2	3.3	3.7	4.6	5.4	2.8	4.4
		35–45	5.8	4.7	4.5	6.2	5.6	3.1	5.6
BLACKS	Hardcore	Female 18–25	5.2	3.4	3.2	3.3	5.3	5.1	5.3
		35–45	7.0	4.9	3.6	4.8	6.0	2.9	6.1
		Male 18–25	6.7	4.0	4.1	5.1	5.7	4.7	6.0
		35–45	6.0	4.8	2.6	3.9	5.6	4.8	5.9
	Working Class	Female 18–25	5.0	4.2	2.9	5.6	5.4	3.3	5.0
		35–45	4.5	4.5	2.3	4.3	5.7	3.4	5.0
		Male 18–25	7.1	5.5	4.2	6.1	6.3	2.9	6.1
		35–45	6.6	4.0	2.7	4.7	5.8	3.8	6.5

Table 12 (Continued)

Independent Variables			Get Respect	Don't Depend on Others	Lazy for a While	Glad Not to Listen to Teachers	Get Job Training	Move into Own Apartment	Treated Better by Parents
	Female	18–25	5.4	4.0	2.7	4.3	5.5	4.5	4.0
		35–45	5.1	3.4	2.9	3.4	5.5	2.5	4.2
Middle Class	Male	18–25	5.9	3.6	3.6	3.8	3.9	3.4	4.7
		35–45	4.9	3.1	2.8	4.0	5.4	2.4	4.4
	Female	18–25	5.9	4.7	3.5	5.4	5.3	4.2	4.8
		35–45	6.4	5.8	2.0	3.7	6.6	3.8	5.4
Hardcore	Male	18–25	5.5	4.4	3.6	4.3	5.4	3.7	5.5
		35–45	7.1	5.3	2.7	3.8	5.6	3.9	5.9
	Female	18–25	5.4	3.9	2.4	4.1	6.9	2.9	3.7
		35–45	5.3	3.1	3.4	4.9	5.8	2.7	5.3
WHITES Working Class	Male	18–25	5.7	3.9	3.7	4.8	6.5	3.5	4.9
		35–45	6.1	3.8	3.4	5.1	5.5	2.6	5.2
	Female	18–25	4.9	3.5	2.7	5.1	5.4	2.8	3.7
		35–45	5.5	3.4	3.1	3.9	5.0	3.3	3.2
Middle Class	Male	18–25	3.2	3.4	4.0	5.2	4.8	3.8	4.2
		35–45	5.2	3.4	2.4	5.0	5.4	2.7	4.4

1. Main effect for race ($p < .0065$): Both univariate and multivariate tests indicate that whites are more likely than blacks to see *buy a car* as a consequence of finishing high school, but blacks are more likely to see *feel proud of yourself* as a consequence. Univariate tests show blacks more likely to see getting *treated better by parents* as a consequence, but this item shares variance with *glad not to listen to teachers*.

2. Main effect for socioeconomic status ($p < .0010$): Univariate and multivariate tests indicate that the hardcore is most likely to see *feel proud of yourself* and *get respect* as consequents of finishing high school (the middle class is least likely). However, members of the middle class are most likely to see *move into own apartment* as a consequence of finishing high school, whereas the hardcore members are least likely to do so. Univariate tests show the hardcore as most likely to see *feel more mature*, *don't depend on others*, and being *treated better by parents* as consequents of finishing high school, with the middle class the least likely to do so. Also, the working class is most likely to see *get job training* as a consequence (the middle class least likely). *Feel more mature* shares variance with *feel proud of yourself*, and *don't depend on others* is related to *get respect*. *Get job training* shares variance with preceding item, and *treated better by parents* shares variance with *move into own apartment*.

3. Main effect for sex ($p < .0002$): Males are more likely than females to see *go into the military*, *buy a car*, and being *treated better by parents* as consequences of finishing high school, according to both univariate and multivariate tests. Multivariate tests indicate variance unique to *feel proud of yourself* (females more likely to see this) as a consequence), *get married* (females more likely to see this), and *get respect* (males more likely to see this). Univariate tests show females more likely to see being able to *plan future* as a consequence of finishing high school; the significance of this is removed by item 5, *feel proud of yourself*.

4. Main effect for age ($p < .0434$): Univariate and multivariate tests indicate that younger people are more likely than older people to see being able to be *lazy for a while* and *move into own apartment* as results of finishing high school. Multivariate tests show that young people are also more likely to see *buy a car* as a result of finishing high school.

5. Race $\times$ sex $\times$ age ($p < .0010$): Univariate and multivariate tests indicate that older white males are most likely to see *get a job* as a result of finishing high school; younger black females are least likely to see this as a consequence. Except for young males, all white age groups are more likely to see this as a consequence than their black counterparts. Young black males are most likely to see *go to college* as a consequence of finishing high school; older black males are least likely to see this as a consequence. For females, each age group of whites is more likely than its black counterpart to see this as a consequence. Young black females are most likely to see *move into own apartment* as a consequence, older black females are least likely to do so. Univariate tests show older white males most likely to see *go into the military* as a consequence, but this appears related to *get a job*. Younger black males are most likely to see *feel more mature* as a consequence of finishing high school, younger white males are least likely. The same holds true for *get respect*. These items lose significance in multivariate tests and appear related most closely with *feel proud of yourself*.

CHAPTER SIX

Eco-System Distrust in the Black Ghetto

H . C . TRIANDIS , J . FELDMAN ,

D . E . WELDON , AND W . HARVEY

To summarize a major segment of the data, we will utilize the concept of "eco-system distrust." By eco-system we mean the environment of an individual, consisting of people, things, institutions, etc. Eco-system trust means that most entities in one's environment are seen as potentially beneficial, and a person sees himself able to act on the environment to make it even more beneficial. Conversely, eco-system distrust means that most entities in the environment are seen as potentially harmful, and the individual does not see himself as able to improve his situation.

We can easily imagine how eco-system distrust can develop when there is an extreme scarcity of resources. Consider a parent who promises something valuable, like a toy, to a child. Lack of resources may make it impossible to deliver the toy. The child learns to distrust such a parent. Thousands of similar experiences can create a general perceptual orientation toward the environment which includes distrust of every aspect of it.

Components of the syndrome include less trust for people, suspicion of the motives of others, rejection of authority figures, a lower degree of certainty that particular events will be followed by other events, a sense of individual powerlessness, and a sense that if one is not terribly careful he will get into trouble.

The implications of this construct for the behavior of the hardcore are important. A person with eco-system distrust will respond to a supervisor with suspicion (which the supervisor may interpret as hostility), will prefer "correct" and formal relations with others to friendly relations, will doubt that his "good" behavior will necessarily lead to a raise, a promotion, or other good outcomes, and hence will not respond to such incentives.

Since this is a general orientation, disconfirmation of any aspect of the orientation will not necessarily change it. One needs to confront the worker during training with a massive disconfirmation as well as self-insight as to the source of his orientation.

EMPIRICAL FINDINGS

The three-mode factor analysis of the stereotype data resulted in findings that are summarized in Tables 1 and 2. One of the dimensions extracted by the three-mode analysis combined responses to the scales *trustworthy, hardworking,* and *helpful.* This factor we call trustworthiness. The tables show that blacks are consistently low on this factor as compared with whites. Only black militants, black men, and hustlers are seen as more *trustworthy* by blacks than by whites.

These results were replicated with the data from the study of behavioral intentions. In Figure 1 we show the mean responses of black hardcore males of Phase III on the *would trust* item for several stimulus persons next to the mean responses of the white middle-class males.

Table 1 Second Subject Point of View Contrasts a Black Majority and a White Majority: Characteristics of five types of people as seen by black and white subjects.

Types of People	White Subjects	Black Subjects of Second Viewpoint
People who rely on force	more go-getting more trustworthy less unimportant	less go-getting less trustworthy more unimportant
People thriving under the system	*	*
Safe, dependable, giving people	*	*
People with status and authority	less cultivated less opportunistic less unimportant more trustworthy	more cultivated more opportunistic more unimportant less trustworthy
Rejected people	less unimportant	more unimpor tan

* No important deviations from neutral attributions.

Table 2 Third Subject Point of View Contrasts a Black Minority and a White Minority

Types of People	White Subjects	Black Subjects
People who rely on force	more go-getting more trustworthy	less go-getting less trustworthy
People thriving under the system	more go-getting more trustworthy	less go-getting less trustworthy
Safe, dependable, giving people	less go-getting	more go-getting
People with status and authority	less go-getting	more go-getting
Rejected people	less go-getting	more go-getting more trustworthy

Note that the slope of the lines is always consistent. This pattern is not due to a response set, since on other kinds of judgments, such as on the *would go out with* scale (Figure 2), there is no such consistency.

To make sure that the reader can see that this pattern of answers is not due to the difference in social class, we show in Figure 3 the same kind of data for the black and white hardcore. The pattern of answers is clearly similar, although the perfect consistency in the slope of the lines is no longer present. The fact that middle-class blacks are more similar to whites than are the hardcore blacks can be seen from Figure 4, where a number of lines are horizontal. In short, blacks are different from whites and the hardcore more than the middle class.

It is also interesting to observe the reactions to the *would trust* scale among black and white men and women to black and white men and women (from Phase III). These data are summarized in Table 3. Note that the ingroup perceptions of the blacks are consistently lower on trust than are the ingroup perceptions of the whites, with one exception: for black men viewing black women. Furthermore, the outgroup perceptions of the blacks are dramatically lower on trust than are those of the whites. Also interesting is the fact that black men trust women more than men; white men trust men more than women. But black women trust men more than women and white women trust women more than men.

A similar pattern of lack of trust emerges in the analysis of role perceptions and the perceptions of the antecedents and consequents of TO DO YOUR OWN THING. Table 4 shows the perceived consequences

Table 3 Trust toward Black and White Men and Women

By	Toward			
	White		Black	
Black	Men	Women	Men	Women
Women	3.7	3.6	5.1	5.2
Men	3.7	4.0	5.0	5.5
White				
Women	5.5	5.6	5.1	5.4
Men	5.3	5.2	4.8	4.7

Table 4 Consequents of TO DO YOUR OWN THING

	Rotated Factor Matrix			
Items	1	2	3	4
Are satisfied with yourself	.96	.34	—.64	.78
Feel free	.70	.51	—.80	.86
Have other people putting you down	.08	—.55	.29	1.76*
Are happy	.42	.65	—.56	.83
Don't depend on others	—.51	.12	.33	1.84*
Have friends	.58	.78	—.40	.54
Have purpose in your life	1.09*	.72	—.11	—.00
Get in trouble	—.11	.29	2.32*	.30
Enjoy life more	1.41*	.79	.18	—.57
Aren't tied down by society	1.65*	—.67	.48	.32
Feel you have done something important	1.84*	.14	—.25	—.32
Are mature (grown up)	2.24*	—.63	.31	—.17
Ignore society's rules	.47	.09	2.12*	.01
Keep trying to make yourself better	—.08	1.75*	.25	—.04
Are responsible for yourself	—.36	2.24*	.27	—.15

1. Self-actualization
2. Responsibility
3. Trouble
4. Independence and rejection by others

Factor Correlation Matrix				
	1	2	3	4
1				
2	0.96			
3	0.76	0.75		
4	0.96	0.95	0.79	

* Highest factor loading.

Table 4 (Continued)

Group Means on Original Factor Scores

Group	1	2	3	4
1	4.11	4.38	.96	3.80
2	4.30	4.00	1.65	4.27
3	4.05	4.00	1.25	3.93
4	3.35	3.40	1.39	3.48

Discriminant Functions

Factors	Function 1	Function 2
1	.6395	−.1994
2	.6531	.5469
3	.1319	−.6537
4	.3836	−.4836
5		
6		
% of variance	69.2	30.2

Group Means on Discriminant Functions

Group	Function 1	Function 2
1	7.08	−.89
2	7.21	−1.81
3	6.88	−1.34
4	5.88	−1.40

Overall F ratio 2.14 $(df = 12,238)$, $p < .05$.

of TO DO YOUR OWN THING (data from Phase II). The data suggest that the middle class responds to TO DO YOUR OWN THING as though it lives in a benign environment, while the lower-class samples feel threatened and believe that they are likely to get into trouble if they do their own thing. The data of Phase III show some samples very high in the perceived connection of TO DO YOUR OWN THING and *get into trouble:* the black males and the middle-class females (both black and white). Our interpretation is that the black males reflect their environment, while the middle-class females use these perceptions as "controls" over their own behavior.

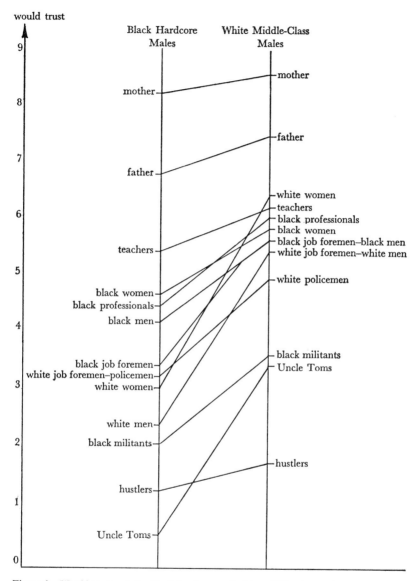

would trust

Figure 1 *Would trust* scale for black hardcore and white middle-class males.

A consequence of eco-system distrust is that reinforcements, either positive or negative, appear disconnected from other events. This pattern is clear when we examine the responses of the hardcore blacks to positive events such as TO GET A GOOD JOB, TO GET PROMOTED, TO GET

A RAISE, TO HAVE YOUR OWN HOUSE, TO NOT DEPEND ON OTHERS, TO
BUY A CAR, and TO BUY FINE CLOTHES. Similar results are suggested
when we examine negative events, such as TO GET A BAD JOB or TO GET
FIRED FROM YOUR JOB.

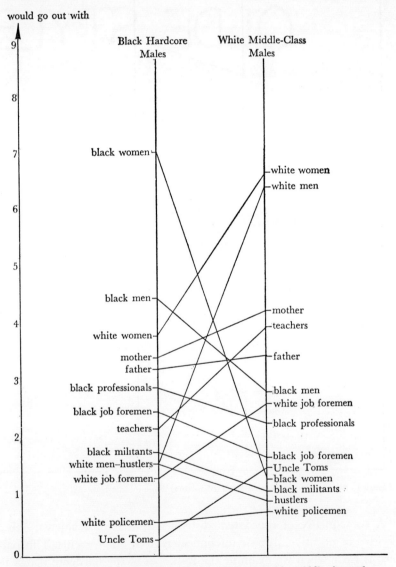

Figure 2 *Would go out with* scale for black hardcore and white middle-class males.

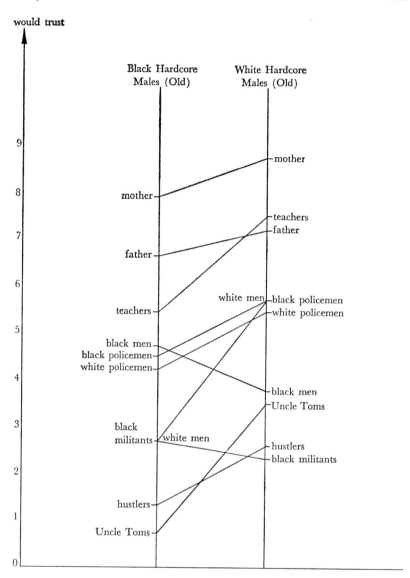

Figure 3 *Would trust* scale for black and white hardcore males.

Differences in the connections between behavior and positive or negative outcomes found in our samples take two forms. First, connections that are ecologically valid, such as the connection between *finish high school* and TO GET A GOOD JOB, are not employed by the hardcore blacks to the same extent as they are by other black samples or by the whites. Second, positive emotional experiences are not expected to be associated with the positive outcomes and negative experiences with the negative outcomes to the same extent as they are for other samples. For example, TO GET A GOOD JOB is not seen by the

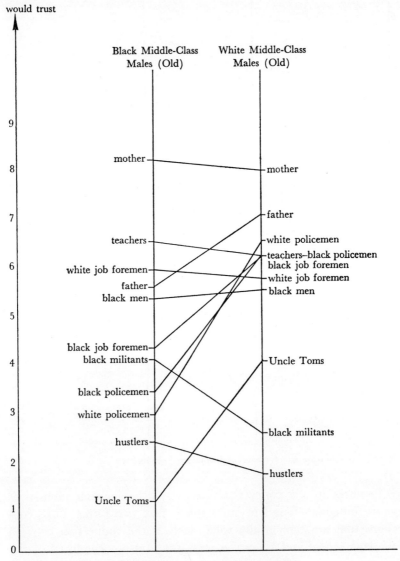

Figure 4   *Would trust* scale for black and white middle-class males.

hardcore as leading to *enjoy work* to the same extent as it is for the other samples.

These general statements are supported by several highly significant findings. We will mention just a few in support of these generalizations. Details can be seen in the microfiche tables.

The hardcore blacks of Phase II are less likely than the other samples to see TO GET PROMOTED being followed by *be proud of yourself, accept more responsibility, make plans for the future, feel safer, get more respect from people, have more money, change your ideas about work,* and *work harder on the new job.* Similarly, they see little connection between TO GET A RAISE and *work harder, want to get ahead even more, make your family happy, feel you have done something worthwhile, want to stay on the job,* and *be proud of your work.* Furthermore, the smaller connection between TO HAVE YOUR OWN HOUSE and *have a better place to raise a family, be happy with it, have privacy, feel safe,* and *have more responsibility* suggests that the hardcore blacks do not see ownership of a house as a positive event, as do the other samples. Similarly, there is a smaller connection between TO BUY A CAR and *be happy,* and between TO BUY FINE CLOTHES and *show yourself off, impress people,* and *go to fancy places.*

Turning to the negative outcomes, we find the black hardcore seeing little connection between *acting like you do not care, have a bad record, be a high school dropout, be fired from your other job, not want to get ahead, be lazy,* or *not look around* and TO GET A BAD JOB, and the latter is not connected as much with *quit* and *be bored.* Furthermore, this sample sees little connection between *disobey the boss, not be dependable, goof off on the job,* and *not get along with other people at work* and TO GET FIRED FROM YOUR JOB, or between *cause an accident, not understand the job, do the job badly, be late all the time, be unreliable,* and *not have any ambition* and TO GET FIRED. It was further found that TO GET FIRED is not strongly connected, for this sample, with *worry, feel embarrassed, look for another job, lose respect for yourself,* and *try to do a better job,* as it is in the other samples.

The lack of connection between events is further seen in the fact that the hardcore see no more reason to "join a revolution" than do other black and white samples.

The specificity of the antecedents and consequents of events is not as great with the black hardcore as it is with other samples. There is

a flavor of greater "appropriateness" of the antecedents and consequents of educational achievements for the other samples than for the
black hardcore. For example, the middle-class samples emphasize *good
grades* and *have no disciplinary problems* as antecedents of TO FINISH
HIGH SCHOOL; the hardcore, and to some extent all black samples,
emphasize *be interested, motivated,* and *intelligent.* Turning to the
consequents, the middle class emphasize tangible consequences such as
buy a car or *move to new apartment,* while the hardcore emphasize
pride and *feel good.* There is a clear pattern of valuing finishing high
school in the middle class which is not found to the same degree among
blacks, and is certainly not present in the hardcore samples. The overlap of the antecedents and consequents found among whites with the
middle class, and blacks with the hardcore, is interesting. It suggests
that certain kinds of values diffuse beyond the social classes or racial
groups in which they originate. Such overlap, in spite of a research
design which renders race and social class independent, suggests that
this is a reliable phenomenon rather than a statistical artifact.

Furthermore, many ghetto blacks see very tense relationships in the
ingroup (e.g., father is more likely to *hit* his son than in other samples).
Friends can be *bad* for you (Triandis, Feldman, and Harvey, 1970,
p. 62); teachers are *unimportant* and *do not deserve respect* (Triandis, Feldman, and Harvey, 1970, pp. 69, 89); ministers are *exploitative* (this is the name of a factor summarizing several behaviors such
as *paid well, fakers, lazy*), and social workers are *unimportant* and
should be *avoided* (Triandis, Feldman, and Harvey, 1970, p. 104).

There is evidence that distrust is a characteristic of some ghetto
blacks (Phase II), and in a mild form this syndrome can also be seen
in the "employable unemployed blacks" (Phase III) and other lower-
class samples.

Consistent with the distrust for the environment is the lack of clarity
in the connections between events. If one does not trust the eco-system
to "work well," he may well see little connection between events. Thus
the blacks from the ghetto studied in Phase II have trouble seeing a
connection between *disobey the boss* and TO GET FIRED FROM YOUR
JOB, or between *skip work* and TO GET FIRED, or between *skip work*
and TO ACQUIRE A BAD REPUTATION. The other samples see clear connections. In general, there is a tendency for the blacks in this sample
to see few connections between what they do and what they get.

In addition, the connections they do see appear to reflect less realistic information on how to get from one state to another (e.g., they fail to see that one must graduate from high school in order to go to college). In short, connections which appear "obvious" to the middle class may simply not be present.

Consistent with the lack of connections just mentioned are the weak or nonexistent connections between reinforcements and other events. This pattern is clear when we examine the responses of the hardcore blacks to such positive events as TO GET A GOOD JOB, TO GET PROMOTED, TO GET A RAISE, TO HAVE YOUR OWN HOUSE, TO NOT DEPEND ON OTHERS, TO BUY A CAR, and TO BUY FINE CLOTHES or to such negative events as TO GET A BAD JOB or TO GET FIRED FROM YOUR JOB. The hardcore blacks see little connection between ecologically valid antecedents and these events (e.g., between *finish high school* and TO GET A GOOD JOB) or between these events and appropriate emotions (e.g., TO GET A GOOD JOB leading to *enjoy work;* TO GET A BAD JOB leading to *quit* or *be bored*).

A striking pattern is that many of the behaviors that lead to desirable goals in the middle-class samples reflect normative determinants ("what we *must* do"); by contrast ghetto blacks of Phase II connect mostly "fun" behaviors to good outcomes. For example, an antecedent of TO FINISH HIGH SCHOOL for the middle class, but not the hardcore, is *get good grades.* For the hardcore a major antecedent is *enjoy school.*

Also consistent with the concept of eco-system distrust is rejection of the establishment. The ghetto blacks of Phase II reject black policemen, black foremen, and black professionals about as much as they reject whites in such roles. Their reactions to stimulus persons associated with the establishment are much more negative than are those of the other samples.

There is a general black rejection of establishment roles. Specifically, the systematic sample data show a race main effect for TEACHERS. They are seen as less *hardworking* by the blacks ($p < .03$). BLACK FOREMEN are seen as less *trustworthy* and less *hardworking* ($p < .0009$). WHITE JOB FOREMEN are less *trustworthy* and *hardworking,* WHITE and BLACK POLICEMEN are less *trustworthy* ($p < .0002$), but BLACK MILITANTS are more *trustworthy, hardworking,* and *intelligent* and less *lazy* ($p < .004$), and UNCLE TOMS are less *trustworthy, hard-*

working, intelligent, important, and *tough* ($p < .0000$) as rated by the black than by the white samples.

When a person feels he is unable to trust the eco-system, he also is likely to feel that he cannot do much to change it, and hence that he is unimportant. Consistent with that are the findings shown in Figure 5. The top section refers to black data (Phase III) and the bottom to white. The social class (hardcore, working class, middle class) and age (18-25 or 35-45) of the samples are also shown. It can be seen that four groups see themselves as relatively low in importance: both the black and white old working class and the two black hardcore samples (young and old). By contrast, the white hardcore subjects do not show this effect.

The cognitive maps we extracted by the procedures described in the Methods section suggest broad similarity across all groups. On some aspects of subjective culture there is a general contrast between all the black and all the white samples. Within this framework of similarity and difference, there are *major* differences in the subjective culture of some ghetto blacks on the one hand and other hardcore, working-class, and middle-class blacks on the other.

To sum up, then, there is a lot of evidence that some ghetto blacks experience eco-system distrust. They distrust people in general, even their ingroup, with the exception of black women, their mothers, and black militants. They see little connection between events. They feel unimportant. They reject the establishment, whether black or white. The manifestations of this phenomenon are sometimes subtle. For example, some of the whites show an acceptance of aggressive-joking relationships that is only possible among people who have established a good interpersonal relationship. The black hardcore adopt a "low profile" — distance and formality — which may protect a bruised self-esteem and reflect their general distrust. The white middle class show an active involvement in interpersonal relationships and also much complexity; for example, a person may be friendly but also critical of others.

The lack of clear connections among events reflects general eco-system distrust but may also reflect reality. The environment of many hardcore blacks *is* unpredictable. Many members of the black hardcore do not control their environment as much as the middle class, since they are dependent on outside agencies (the police, welfare agencies,

etc.). The social structure may be less stable. There is a certain value
stretch (Rodman, 1963) which allows for certain forms of behavior
and social organization that are not acceptable among the middle class
to be considered acceptable in the ghetto.

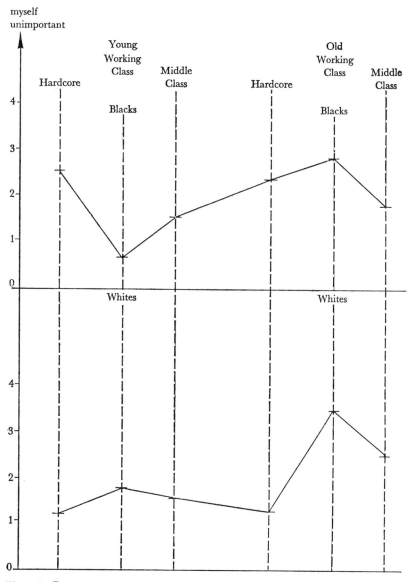

Figure 5   Responses of six samples to importance of self (Phase III)

A most interesting difference was obtained in reactions of the samples to TO DO YOUR OWN THING. The lower-class males, as well as the hardcore samples, seem to think that one consequence will be *get into trouble*. The middle class see self-improvement and self-actualization themes connected with this concept, though the females also see trouble. Our interpretation is that the environment of the middle class is designed by middle-class males for the middle class; if they do their own thing, it is good for them. The environment of the ghetto is a consequence of exploitative economic conditions. It is not designed by the ghetto dwellers and it is not good for anybody. Doing your own thing in that environment leads to trouble.

What are the implications of these findings for race relations? First, the distrust of blacks for whites, particularly white men, suggests that any behavior of a white man might be "misinterpreted" by blacks. If a white man smiles, the black man may think, "He is trying to trip me"; if he tries to help, the black man may say, "He does it because the government forced him." Whites have to learn to emit behaviors that are sufficiently consistent and clear that they cannot be misinterpreted by blacks. This will require the development of new skills.

Second, whites must learn that establishment roles are likely to be rejected by blacks. The fact that a policeman is black does not make him that much more acceptable than a white policeman.

The highly negative, cynical, and competitive view of interpersonal relationships in some of the black ghetto samples and their low sense of importance are particularly inappropriate for life in a modern industrial society. Modern environments require cooperation. The most striking characteristic of modern times, as contrasted with life a few hundred years ago, is the size of institutions: large industry, large armies, large cities, large educational systems, etc. Such institutions assume that people will cooperate, conform, and "adjust" to rules set by the leadership of the institutions. But a person who looks at interpersonal relationships as zero-sum games (if *he* wins something, *I* will lose the same) is not a "good" member of such institutions. Nor are such institutions good for a person with low self-esteem who can be discouraged easily and "drop out." Such institutions do not have the means to "counsel," "support," and help an individual with low self-esteem. Thus eco-system distrust and large social organizations are in some respects incompatible.

CHAPTER SEVEN

Reactions to Self, Ingroup, Outgroups, and the Establishment

H . C . T R I A N D I S , J . F E L D M A N ,
D . E . W E L D O N , A N D W . H A R V E Y

In this chapter we shall examine data that suggest characteristic ways in which black hardcore samples react to the self, members of their ingroup, their outgroups, and particularly the establishment.

We shall begin with an examination of self-perceptions, including suggestions that these samples prefer to present themselves to others as "powerful" rather than "nice" and show more acceptance of the conditions of the ghetto than do other samples. These may be viewed as highly positive aspects of adjustment to the difficult ghetto environment. We will then turn to relations within the ingroup. We will note some preference for mother over father, some greater emphasis on informality in both ingroup and work roles, and a considerable rejection of establishment roles.

Before presenting these data, it is important to summarize the extent to which the points of view that we are to describe are shared with other samples. First, the hardcore blacks have a point of view that they often share with hardcore whites. By contrast, working-class blacks often have a viewpoint like that of the middle-class whites. However, whether the overlap is with the white lower class or middle class depends on the particular topics. When the black hardcore share a point of view with another sample, it is usually with the other black samples. The black working class, however, sometimes overlap with the white middle class, particularly when we consider their conceptions of what happens in order TO GET ALONG WITH THE BOSS, TO GET ALONG WITH PEOPLE AT WORK, and TO HAVE DIGNITY. For example, for the middle-class whites and working-class blacks dignity is associated with positive personal characteristics, while the black hardcore see it as a "pose."

THE SELF, INGROUP, AND OUTGROUPS

We begin our overview with a consideration of six sets of stimulus persons, obtained empirically.

I.   Ingroup — my mother, my father.
II. Policemen — white and black.
III. Uncle Toms.
IV. I, myself.
V.   People with status and authority—teachers, black professionals.
VI. Rejected people — black militants, black men.

Figure 1 summarizes the reactions on the evaluation and unimportance dimensions of the four samples of Phase II. In Phase II we did not study "I, myself"; hence there is no entry for that concept.

Looking at Figure 1, we note at once that the black hardcore consistently devaluate and rate as more unimportant the ingroup, police, Uncle Toms, and people with status and authority. Only the stimulus persons that are rejected by the mainstream are seen by the black hardcore as higher in evaluation than they are by other samples, but even they are still seen as more unimportant than is the case for other samples. These results are replicated for Phase III only for Uncle Toms (see Figure 2a). The black hardcore see "I, myself" as much more unimportant than do the subjects in the other sample (see Figure 2b).

The hardcore of Phase II were seeking help from a drug addiction clinic, while those of Phase III were employable unemployed selected by a survey research organization for inclusion in the sample. It seems reasonable to assume that the Phase II hardcore were more extreme in their failure to effectively adjust to their environment, since they asked for help to cope with it. The consistency of the results across the two samples suggests that the hardcore are likely to feel that the self, ingroup, and "people like me" are at least somewhat unimportant.

REACTIONS TO THE SELF

There is a theme that runs through several of the findings. The hardcore blacks often express it in forms that can be summarized by the

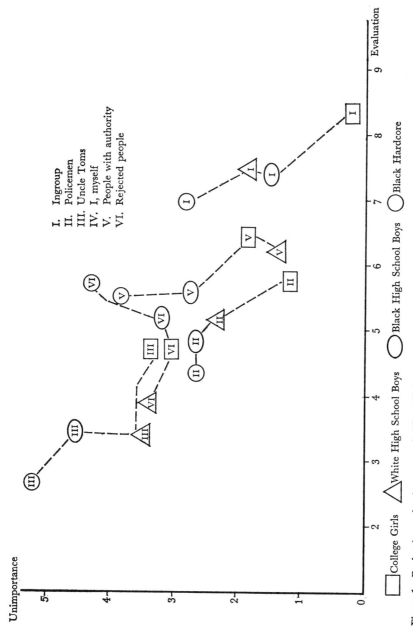

Figure 1 Evaluation and unimportance in Phase II data.

Unimportance

Evaluation

I.   Ingroup
II. Policemen
III. Uncle Toms
IV. I, myself
V.   People with authority
VI. Rejected people

☐ College Girls   △ White High School Boys   ⬭ Black High School Boys   ◯ Black Hardcore

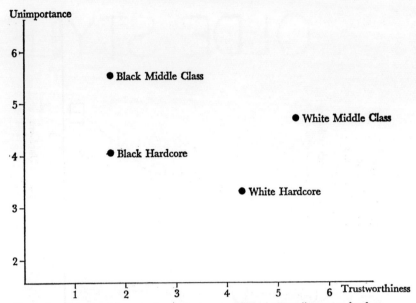

Figure 2a Trustworthiness and unimportance of "Uncle Toms" as seen by four samples of old males (Phase III).

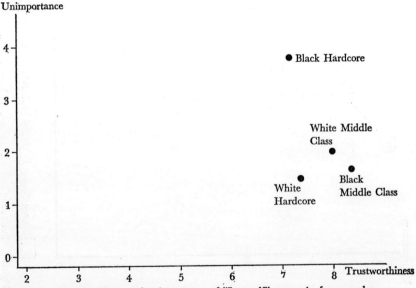

Figure 2b Trustworthiness and unimportance of "I, myself" as seen by four samples of old males (Phase III).

idea: "Being powerful is more important than being nice." The suggestion is that life in the ghetto is highly competitive. One wins not by being nice, which is in part a white middle-class point of view particularly strongly held by the counterculture, but by having power.

Interpersonal relations in the ghetto appear to be conceived more often than not as a struggle. Furthermore, you get to the top by having the right "pose," i.e., wearing fine clothes, "rapping," and having a "good line." The theme emerges again in the responses to the concept TO BE RESPECTED. The ghetto sees less connection than does the middle class between the antecedents to *be kind to others, respect yourself, like other people, be willing to help others, be honest, be thoughtful, respect other people, be modest, be trustworthy, act friendly to others,* and *be generous with what you have* and TO BE RESPECTED AND ADMIRED BY OTHERS. Furthermore, the antecedents of TO HAVE GOOD FRIENDS suggest that the hardcore see less of a connection than do the middle-class samples between *listen to their ideas, choose friends wisely, keep others' secrets, do things for them,* and *be reliable, loyal,* and *helpful* with having good friends.

Among the consequents of TO HAVE GOOD FRIENDS are the ideas *do things together, have fun, help them if they need it, give things to each other, trust them, feel safe, feel good, share what you have, be loyal,* and *get respect.* These ideas are again emphasized by the middle class and de-emphasized by the ghetto samples, who instead emphasize that *you get in trouble together.*

There is a strong tendency for the middle class to see TO HAVE DIGNITY caused by the following: *respect yourself, be independent, have a good job, be educated, stand up for your ideas, believe in yourself, be proud of yourself,* and *be modest.* These themes are de-emphasized by the ghetto blacks, who instead emphasize *conform to society, dress well, be well known,* and *don't show emotion* as antecedents of TO HAVE DIGNITY.

The extent to which interpersonal relations involve a "pose" is suggested by the antecedents of TO BUY FINE CLOTHES. The middle class samples emphasize *have money, know how to budget your money, have good taste, have a job;* the hardcore emphasize *want to impress people, want to impress women,* and *think that clothes will help you get ahead.* The consequents show a tendency for the middle class to emphasize *go to fancy places, meet more women, get compliments from people,* and *look respectable,* while the hardcore blacks emphasize *are proud of yourself, get ahead at work,* and *believe more in yourself.*

The same themes appear in the antecedents of TO GET A GIRLFRIEND (OR BOYFRIEND). The middle class emphasize *be friendly to everyone, respect yourself, be willing to sacrifice for another person, respect the other person,* and *be yourself (not phony),* while the black samples, particularly the ghetto, emphasize *have a good line (rap, be cool).* The consequences also show a contrast, with the middle class seeing a strong connection and the black hardcore a weak connection between TO GET A GIRLFRIEND and *try to treat her well, have someone to help with your problems, feel more confident, be happy,* and *lose some of your freedom,* as well as *think about getting married.*

In short, the middle class samples emphasize desirable habits while the ghetto samples emphasize a "pose" as determinants of acquiring a girlfriend.

It can be argued that both the emphasis on power and the "pose" are realistic and highly desirable defense mechanisms that improve the chances of adjustment under the difficult conditions of the ghetto. Similarly, the greater acceptance of the conditions of the ghetto, which we will now document, seems to be a factor that improves the chances of adjustment.

There is a reliable difference $(p < .01)$ among the samples on the perceived antecedents of TO BE ROBBED. Specifically, in Phase II the white high school students see a strong connection, while the white female college sample sees a weak connection, between *dress well, go out of your own neighborhood, carry a gun,* and *be tough* and TO BE ROBBED. The two black samples are intermediate. The black hardcore do not see a connection between *get drunk, flash your money around,* and *have a lot of expensive things* and TO BE ROBBED, while the other samples, particularly the high school students of both races, see these as very strong connections. The black hardcore does see a connection between *have friends, lock your house,* and *carry a gun* and TO BE ROBBED, which is not the case with the college sample.

There is also a reliable difference $(p < .01)$ in the consequents. The blacks see a strong connection between TO BE ROBBED and *carry a gun or knife;* the college sample does not see such a connection. The hardcore see a connection between TO BE ROBBED and *go to the doctor for*

treatment, try to collect on insurance, and a low connection between
TO BE ROBBED and *get angry, lose valuable things,* or *don't go out alone
at night any more.*

In short, there is more acceptance of being robbed among the hardcore (less anger, less loss of valuables, less willingness to change one's
style of life). This suggests first that people who do not have valuable
things do not worry about being robbed as much as people who do,
and second that they believe that if you give signals of cautiousness —
carry a gun, lock your door — you might get into trouble. Finally, the
connection between having friends and being robbed suggests a lack
of trust in the friendship network among the hardcore blacks.

The hardcore blacks see very little connection between TO GET AR-
RESTED and *have trouble getting a job, try to tell the police you are
innocent, tell your friends what happened, are always being watched,
go to jail, have a police record, put up bail money, feel guilty,* and *be
embarrassed.* They differ much from the black high school students
who are high on *have trouble getting a job, tell you are innocent,* and
tell your friends, as well as on *go to jail, have a police record,* and *put
up bail money;* they are also different from the college sample, who
feels being arrested leads to *feel guilty* and *embarrassed.* The college
sample is also high on *have to find money for a lawyer, call your family for help,* and *stop doing whatever got you arrested.* The white high
school students are very high on *get beaten up by the police* and *be
put on probation* as consequents of TO GET ARRESTED.

Thus the hardcore do not see diminished chances of getting a job as
a consequence of the arrest (they have no job anyway, even when they
are not arrested), they see no point telling the police they are innocent
(presumably this is because either they are less likely to be innocent or
they feel less able to convince the police even when they are innocent),
they see less likelihood of being watched and less certainty about going
to jail, and they would feel less guilty and embarrassed (the latter
being, presumably, middle-class reactions to being arrested).

The white samples see a stronger connection between *be looking for
"something for nothing"* and TO GAMBLE than do the black samples.
The black hardcore sample seems somewhat positively disposed and
the white high school sample seems most opposed to gambling. The
black high school sample is also negative, as is the college sample.

There are differences both in the antecedents ($p < .01$) and the consequents ($p < .01$) of TO USE DRUGS (ANY ILLEGAL DRUGS). The college sample sees *have money* and *have nerve (guts)* as antecedents to a greater extent than the high school samples; *be unhappy with your life, have friends who use drugs,* and *want new experiences* are emphasized by the white high school students. The college sample sees *have a connection, have nerve, have people telling you how good drugs are, know how to use the drugs, have a safe place to take them, be curious about them,* and *have drugs easily available to you* as antecedents of TO USE DRUGS to a greater extent than the other samples, particularly the hardcore blacks. The hardcore blacks see little connection between *feel inferior* and *be unhappy* and TO USE DRUGS, while the other samples see a connection; the hardcore also see little connection between *not be able to handle your own problems, want to find yourself,* and *want some kicks* and TO USE DRUGS, while the black high school sample sees a strong connection.

On the consequents of TO USE DRUGS, we note that the white high school and the black hardcore samples see TO USE DRUGS followed by *understand things better* and *improve your life,* but this is not so for the other samples. The high school samples are high on *get high, try to get others to use them,* and *escape from your problems,* as well as on *feel sick, spend all your money on them,* and *lose others' respect.*

Thus the white high school sample and black hardcore seem more positively inclined to use drugs, but both high school samples seem extremely ambivalent.

There are dependable ($p < .05$) differences among the samples on the antecedents and also ($p < .01$) on the consequents of TO STEAL. The two samples that have previously been found to have a middle-class viewpoint (the college and the black high school) have strong connections between *want to make easy money, need money,* and *have the chance to do it* and TO STEAL; the white high school and black hardcore see weak connections. All samples with the exception of the black hardcore see strong connections between *have friends that steal, have enough nerve,* and *be stupid* and TO STEAL, but this is not the case with the black hardcore. The black high school students see a strong connection between *want to "improve yourself"* and TO STEAL, but this is not true for the other samples.

Turning to the consequents, we note that the college sample is very high on *feel guilty, be afraid of getting caught,* and *lose friends' respect if they find out.* This is not the case with the other samples. The black high school students see a strong connection between TO STEAL and *hide from the police, steal again, get sent to prison,* and *ruin your chances for a good life if you are caught.* The black hardcore are unusually low in seeing a connection between TO STEAL and *make your family feel bad, lose friends' respect,* and *ruin your chances for a good life if you are caught.* The white high school sample is very high on seeing *have money you need to live* and *can buy things you want* as consequents.

Thus, consistent with earlier findings, we note that the white high school sample and the black hardcore do not feel the sorts of inhibitions that are reported by the college sample. In fact, the social pressures against stealing are practically nonexistent for the hardcore sample. The black high school sample is somewhat ambivalent but generally closer to the inhibited side of the continuum.

The more or less matter-of-fact reaction to TO HAVE FRIENDS and TO DO YOUR OWN THING, which the hardcore see connected with *get into trouble,* suggests further that there is a certain acceptance of the conditions of the ghetto. We believe that these findings indicate that the ghetto hardcore blacks have developed mechanisms that improve their chances of adjustment to the ghetto. Of course, one can wonder to what extent such defenses are "healthy" and to what extent they might produce problems for the individual. For example, there is some evidence that black hardcore samples rate themselves as more intelligent than do other samples. Figure 3 shows some relevant data. Note that in the case of whites, the middle class rates the self as more intelligent, the working-class males are intermediate, and the hardcore rate themselves as less intelligent. This does not happen in the black data. The young blacks rate themselves as intelligent as does the white middle class, no matter what their position on the socioeconomic ladder. The old black middle-class sample rates itself about the same way as the white middle class, but the old working-class black males and the old hardcore black females rate themselves as higher than the black middle class. The slopes of the lines are sharply negative, suggesting that the black working class and hardcore samples react defensively to this rating, while the middle class is "realistic."

A suggestion of defensiveness is also seen in the ratings of self on the *lazy* scale (Figure 4). Note the tendency of the whites to rate themselves more lazy the higher their social class. This is less pronounced in the black data, although a trend exists. The hardcore, presumably because they are not working, are more sensitive to this rating than the other groups.

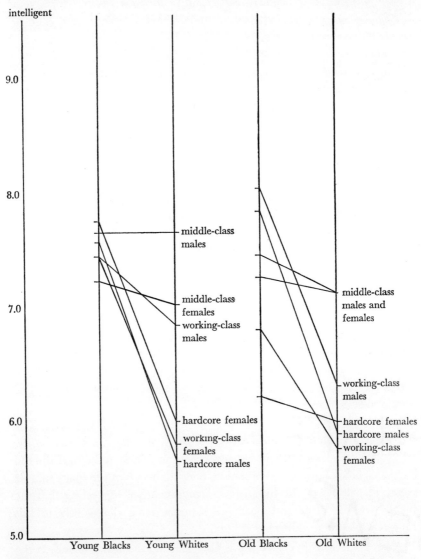

Figure 3   Ratings of "I, myself" on *intelligent* scale.

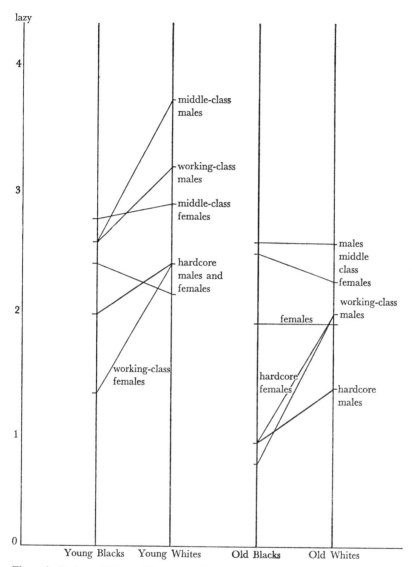

Figure 4 Ratings of "I, myself" on *lazy* scale.

Of course, as is the case with most interpretations, they can be countered by other arguments. For example, a black psychologist might interpret these data (Figure 3) as follows: Among whites there is a subjective reaction to the rating of *intelligent* that is consistent with

objective results such as those obtained in tests of intelligence of different occupational groups. Among blacks, because of discrimination,
there is no such differentiation of intelligence by occupational groups.
To put it differently: An intelligent white with a hardcore background
would become middle class, hence "move out" of his class. This cannot
happen to a black because he is discriminated against. Hence the mean
intelligence of blacks from different social classes is about the same,
a fact which is reflected in their subjective ratings. Furthermore, a
person who can get along well in the ghetto may see himself as intelligent ("smart"), regardless of his I.Q.; and what is more, he probably
is intelligent, since I.Q. tests tend to measure middle-class skills.

Such a defensive self-rating may produce difficulties in adjusting to
a job, where a person might be expected to show modesty. We note, in
the data on job perceptions, that black hardcore samples reject jobs
that they are not capable of doing more than do other samples. This
is presumably a "sour grapes" effect which may help in adjustment.
However, there are also reports that blacks who are low in self-esteem
stay in jobs longer than blacks who are high in self-esteem (Rosen,
1969). The point is that, given the poor jobs available for unskilled
blacks in American industry today, one might be better off with a low
self-esteem. This is, of course, a sad commentary on our society. It
says that we have environments in which "sick" people can adjust
better than "healthy" people.

This same issue can be seen in the differences in the perceptions of
the antecedents and consequents of TO FINISH HIGH SCHOOL. We find
the white samples emphasizing realistic antecedents, such as *attendance, good grades,* and *personal maturity,* while the blacks, particularly the hardcore, see unusual qualities, such as high *intelligence,
motivation,* and *interest,* necessary for high school graduation. Furthermore, the consequents for the whites are specific, such as *buy a new
car,* while for the black hardcore they are emotional: *feel proud, feel
good.* One could argue that the lack of specificity in the perceived
antecedents and consequents is responsible for some of the observed
differences between blacks and whites in the probability that they will
drop out of high school. This could be said to be a "psychological
weakness" among the blacks; but one could equally argue that when a
society does not have enough jobs for one group, it does not provide
the conditions for the development of perceptions of specific anteced-

ents and consequents. Hence it is the state of the society that is reflected in these data.

This phenomenon is seen again and again in our data. For example, TO JOIN A UNION is less frequently connected with the antecedents *learn a trade* or *finish high school* by the blacks than by the whites, and more frequently connected with *know somebody* by the blacks than by the whites. Given that it has been true that many blacks who learned a trade did not necessarily get a job, and many who finished high school did not get one, it is realistic for blacks to see less connection between these events and TO JOIN A UNION. Furthermore, given the difficulty in joining a union if one is not sponsored by a union member, and given the small number of blacks in some unions, it is again realistic to emphasize *know somebody* as an antecedent of TO JOIN A UNION, as was found among the blacks.

One way to summarize these points is as follows. Although from the perspective of white middle-class society some of the views of the black hardcore are unrealistic, defensive, or "sick," from the perspective of an analysis of the kind of society to which blacks are trying to adjust, the very same characteristics and viewpoints are realistic, adjustive, and "healthy." Thus, going back to the argument that one finds in the literature between the proponents of model 1, which argues that black society is maladaptive, model 2, which argues that the white establishment is "sick," and model 3, which views both as partially healthy and partially disfunctional, one must argue that these data are more consistent with the second model, although parts of the third can also be supported.

REACTIONS TO THE INGROUP

Two major themes emerge from our data. First, black responses appear much more matrifocal than is the case with whites; second, there is much more informality in ingroup roles among blacks than there is among whites. These points hold for all blacks, not only the black hardcore. Specifically, our study of the concept MOTHER revealed a race effect. That is, blacks are more favorable toward this concept than are whites, since they see her as more *trustworthy, intelligent,* and *aggressive* (in the "go-getting" sense) than do the whites. A possible interpretation of the more positive view of MOTHER in both Phases II and III is that black mothers play a more significant role in family life. More of them work than do mothers in white families. Also, more black families are "headed" by black women.

In the data of Phase II FATHER was seen as less *trustworthy, intelligent,* and *important* and more *aggressive* by the blacks than by the whites ($p < .003$). The hardcore blacks were even more extreme than the high school blacks. However, there was no race effect in the data from Phase III.

The behavioral intentions also show that blacks are more positive toward their mothers than are whites; however, they also show a "reverence" theme, according to which they are less willing to *go out with* and *criticize.*

Blacks, when compared with whites, show more distance from their fathers; i.e., they seem to *respect* and to show less willingness to *criticize* their fathers (in the behavioral intentions data). This is particularly true for the middle-class and the hardcore black samples.

Figure 5 shows the perceptions of four ingroup roles among the black and white hardcore young males and the white middle-class older males. They indicate more role differentiation on the Superordination dimension for the middle class (*discipline* and *give orders to*) and a greater tendency toward informality (*play games with*) in the hardcore data.

Informal relations are here conceived as reflecting greater willingness to express oneself openly, hence, more likelihood that the parties will *fight* and *hit* but also *love, admire* and *play games with.* The one exception to the generalization of greater informality in the hardcore data is found in the responses to the *call him Mr. (her Mrs.)* scale, where the hardcore are higher. However, this seems to be a scale that may express love more than formality; i.e., it may reflect positive affect rather than social distance. In three out of four of the ingroup roles of Figure 5, the blacks have a significantly larger tendency to *call Mr. (Mrs.)* than the whites. Social class effects do not reach significance.

In order to understand how this scale is used, we have plotted the responses to *call him Mr. (her Mrs.)* in Figure 6 together with the responses to the *love* scale. We note that the relationship is curvilinear for both the hardcore blacks and whites and the middle-class whites. This was found also in a study of the relationship between formal behavior and associative-dissociative behaviors among Americans and

Greeks (Triandis, Vassiliou, and Nassiakou, 1968). The data showed there too that intimate behaviors (e.g., hit) occur when there is much love *or* hate; formal behaviors occur in situations that are affectively more neutral.

The *call Mr.* scale, then, has the characteristics of a formal behavior. However, note the smaller differentiation of ingroup (mean about 2) and work roles (mean about 3.4) for the hardcore, while the corresponding middle-class role perceptions have means of .5 and 2.5 respectively. In short, the hardcore data differ by about 1.4 scale units

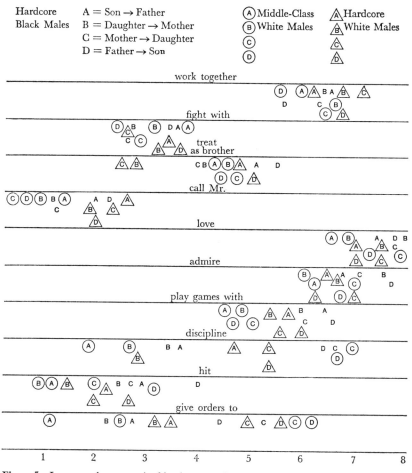

Figure 5 Ingroup roles as perceived by three samples.

on the *call Mr.* scale, while the middle-class data differ by about 2.0 units.

We interpret these findings as follows. For both blacks and whites, hardcore or middle class, the *call him Mr.* (*her Mrs.*) scale implies two qualities: positive affect and formality. However, in the black and the hardcore samples the weight for positive affect is much greater than is the weight for formality, while the reverse is true for the white middle-class sample, where the behavior implies formality to a greater extent than it implies love. Since the blacks and the hardcore have an

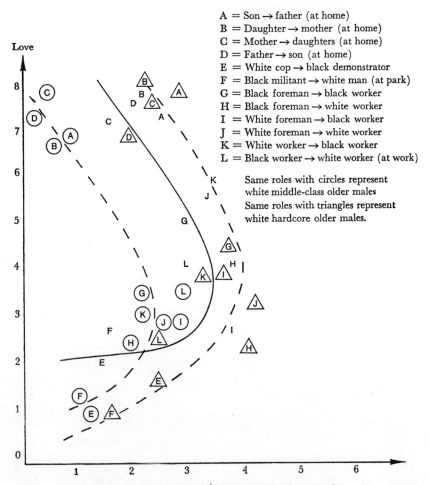

A = Son → father (at home)
B = Daughter → mother (at home)
C = Mother → daughters (at home)
D = Father → son (at home)
E = White cop → black demonstrator
F = Black militant → white man (at park)
G = Black foreman → black worker
H = Black foreman → white worker
I = White foreman → black worker
J = White foreman → white worker
K = White worker → black worker
L = Black worker → white worker (at work)

Same roles with circles represent white middle-class older males
Same roles with triangles represent white hardcore older males.

Figure 6 Relationship of *love* to *call him Mr.* (*her Mrs.*) for three samples.

attenuated relationship between formality and the meaning of *call Mr.*, the difference in the means for ingroup and work roles is smaller for these groups.

Now, if this interpretation of the meaning of *call Mr.* is correct, the "anomalous" finding that blacks and the hardcore see *call Mr.* as more appropriate in ingroup roles than do the middle class disappears. Namely, the blacks and the hardcore see *call Mr.* as more appropriate because this shows greater affect, not because it shows more formality. The total picture of ingroup role perceptions now emerges as one in which the blacks and the hardcore see more informal relations in the ingroup, i.e., more "playing" and less superordination or subordination.

PERCEPTIONS OF WORK RELATIONSHIPS

A primary concern in this project was the study of the perception of the relationships between black and white foremen and black and white workers. There is a general trend in the data obtained in both Phases II and III for the blacks to perceive the WHITE FOREMAN as more superordinate (i.e., bossy) than do the whites. Figure 7 was prepared from the data of the systematic sample (Phase III) to compare the responses of black and white hardcore young males and white middle-class older males (the prototypical samples of hardcore workers and white foremen).

A glance at this figure suggests that the samples differ on the perceived appropriateness of *work together*, with the whites rating it higher than the blacks. On the behaviors *fight with* and *hit* there is also a systematic difference, with the hardcore seeing this type of behavior as more appropriate than did the middle class. On *treat as a brother* the hardcore were higher than the middle class, and there is a similar trend for *love, call Mr.,* and *admire*. Finally, there is a great difference between hardcore and middle class on *give orders to*.

One generalization that emerges from the data we have just reviewed is that the hardcore see greater intimacy and informality in foreman-worker relationships than do the middle class. Intimacy allows both the expression of hostility (*fight with, hit*) and exchanges of love and admiration; it also suppresses the formality of "giving orders." The only finding that is inconsistent with this generalization is the difference on *call him Mr.* However, if we recall that the blacks and the hardcore have a general tendency to give a higher response on this

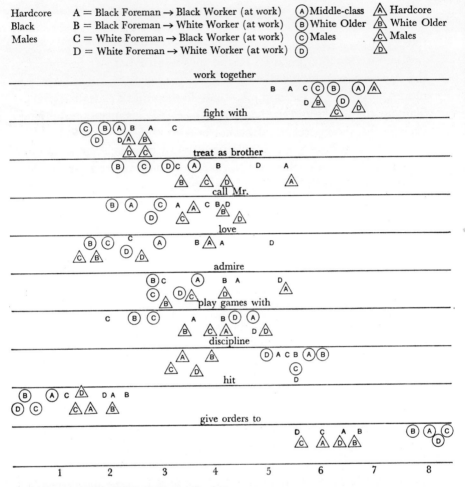

Figure 7 Work roles as perceived by three samples.

scale, particularly in intimate (ingroup) roles, this exception also falls into place.

The only racial difference in this data is that whites expect more harmonious (*work together*) foreman-worker relations than do blacks. Turning to the next figure (Figure 8), which shows the perceived relations between black and white workers, we note a black tendency to see such relations as more intimate. They see open expression of conflict (*fight with, hit*) as more likely but also *treat as brother, love,* and *admire* and even *discipline* as more likely.

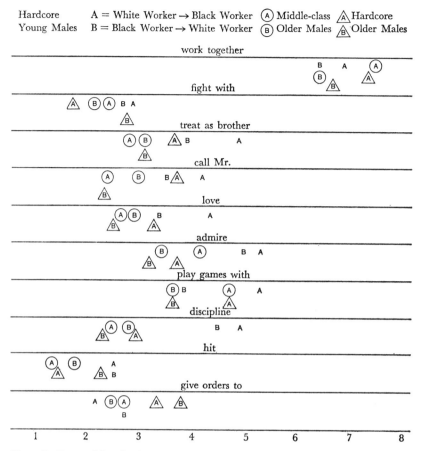

Figure 8   Interracial work roles as perceived by three samples.

A more detailed examination shows that the black hardcore and white middle class are much more similar in their perceptions of the white foreman–black worker relationship than they are in their perceptions of the other work roles. This is hopeful, since this is the one relationship which is most common in industry today and which is likely to continue to be common for a few more years.

Large discrepancies are seen in the perception of the white foreman–white worker relationship, with the blacks more likely to see *treat as brother, call him Mr.,* and *love* as occurring in that role. In short, they see favoritism on the part of white foremen for white workers. This is also seen by comparing roles C and D. The hardcore blacks see more *fight with,* less *treat as brother,* less *love,* less *admire,* much less *play games with* and more *discipline* in the white foreman–black worker role than in the white foreman–white worker role. By contrast, the white middle-class samples see much less difference between the C and D roles, with the exception of the *play games with* scale, on which their data are very similar to the responses of the blacks. Both samples see a better relationship between a black foreman and a black worker than a black foreman and a white worker.

An interesting interaction occurs on the *love* and *admire* scales. Both the blacks and the whites see an actor of their own race as less prejudiced than an actor of the other race, i.e., as more willing to give equal amounts of love to a black or white worker than is the case with an actor of the other race.

The major finding, then, is the hardcore perceptions of greater intimacy in work relations. Such a perception is likely to be derived from conceptions of foreman-worker relations as similar to father-son relations and worker-worker relations as similar to brother-brother relations.

One way to check the generalization that the hardcore see work and ingroup roles as more similar is to examine the way father-son and foreman-worker relations are perceived. In Figure 9 we have shown these data (and also the data for son-father). The hypothesis requires that the distance between the B and C roles for the hardcore be smaller than the distance between the B and C roles for the middle class. In nine out of ten comparisons this is true.

Role differentiation occurs when roles that are learned in the family are transferred to other relations and become different from the original roles (Foa, Triandis, and Katz, 1966). Such differentiation requires experience with different kinds of roles. It is here suggested that this is one area in which both hardcore samples should be trained, since the organization of large-scale industry requires greater differentiation among roles.

The greater informality perceived by the hardcore in work roles, and the greater perceived similarity between work roles and corresponding family roles found in this sample, suggest that work relations appear more like family relations for the hardcore than for the middle class. Consistent with this generalization are the perceived antecedents and consequents of work-related events. For example, TO SKIP WORK

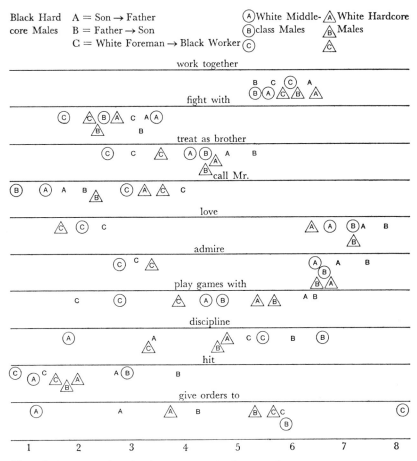

Figure 9   Ingroup and work roles as perceived by three samples.

OR TO LEAVE EARLY (OFTEN) is associated with *have more fun* in the hardcore black sample and less strongly associated with *feel guilty, lose the trust of others,* and *try to make up for it* in the black hardcore than in the middle-class white samples.

Consider the contrast between the home situation and the job; one could easily see that for both whites and blacks not coming home or not being there on time might cause less guilt and would be less associated with *losing trust of others* and *trying to make up for it* than would skipping work or leaving early. Thus the black hardcore responses make sense when seen as responses to an informal situation like that of the family. One shows up when convenient, one leaves when he likes; one does not show up when he feels like it. The whole black hardcore reaction to the work situation is more casual.

Following this line of analysis, we now see that it makes sense that the black hardcore make little connection between TO GOOF OFF ON YOUR JOB and other events, such as *lose others' respect, friendship, get a reputation for being lazy*, etc. The general tendency of the black hardcore to see little connection between poor behavior on the job (e.g., to goof off) and unfavorable social outcomes, or good behavior on the job (e.g., do your job well) and favorable outcomes (good record, satisfaction, promotion), may be, in part, a reaction to the perceived informality of the work situation.

On the other hand, this is not the complete story. There is also a certain amount of cynicism in the responses of the black hardcore which is not derivable from the hypothesis that work relationships are seen as similar to the family relationships. For example, the hardcore blacks see that getting along with the boss, or with others in the work situation, has either mysterious causes (weak antecedents) or requires ingratiation (e.g., play up to the boss, gossip, agree with the boss), and the consequences are favoritism on the part of the boss (get better conditions, more pay, promotion). This pattern is not seen in other samples. No doubt the hardcore, in their brief encounters with work situations, have had traumatic experiences which led to this sort of cynicism.

Thus two themes emerge: the greater informality and intimacy perceived in social relations in work settings and the greater cynicism among the hardcore as contrasted with the white middle class.

REACTIONS TO THE ESTABLISHMENT

Nowhere is the difference in the perceptions of blacks and whites stronger than in their reactions to the establishment roles and institutions and to people who do well under the status quo. Here blacks reject the establishment more clearly than do whites. The establishment is here seen as the police, the foremen, and others who do well under the status quo.

The systematic sample gave data concerning distrust of the police which can be considered quite extraordinary. In most civilized countries the police have a "good press," and the result is a good deal of trust for it. It is really shocking to see how widespread distrust of the police is in Chicago, where the data of Phase III were collected. Of course, this may be just a local condition and may reflect corruption which has often been found in the Chicago police force. Furthermore, the data were collected just a few months after the police were accused by many of eliminating the local leadership of the Black Panthers in a raid that occurred in the early hours of the morning. But even given this extraordinary set of circumstances, it is difficult to believe that the discrepancies in the reactions of the young and the old are due to the treatment of the police by the press. It must be that these two groups have different experiences with law officers.

Table 1 shows the results. Keeping in mind that 4.5 is the neutral point, we find distrust of the police in *all* the black middle-class male samples and *all* the young black male samples. This is too much of a pattern to have occurred by chance. Further, all the young *white* males, with the exception of the working class, show the same distrust. The stimulus WHITE POLICEMAN is rejected on the *trust* scale by all black samples, except the old hardcore females, the old working class, and the young middle-class females. These particular samples also indicate considerable trust of black policemen. The police have the best image among working-class whites and the older white samples.

Given that distrust of the police is so widespread, it is easy to see why criminals can have a field day. It means that the police are unable to get help from citizens. It is also important to note that the ratings of white and black policemen are very similar. It is the role, not the race, that is rejected. Table 2 shows the rated respect toward black foremen and policemen and white foremen and policemen. Figure 10 presents the same data. The right part of the figure shows the way black foremen and white foremen (circles) and black foremen and black policemen (x marks) were rated by the 24 samples of Phase III and the four samples of Phase II. It is obvious that the circles are much more closely located at the 45° line than are the x marks. This means that there is greater similarity in the ratings of the two kinds of foremen than in the ratings of blacks who have different roles.

The left side of the figure shows the locations of the points for black policemen and white policemen (circles). Although the correlation between these two ratings is not as high as it is for foreman, it is easy to see that it is substantial. This correlation could be compared with the ratings for black policemen and foremen (x marks), which are somewhat less well correlated.

In short, the generalization that the role rather than the race determines the ratings holds for both roles.

Table 1   Tendency to Trust Policemen

				Who Are	
	Obtained from			White	Black
BLACKS	Hardcore	Females	Y	3.9	4.4
			O	5.1	6.1
		Males	Y	2.7	2.7
			O	4.3	4.6
	Working Class	Females	Y	5.4	7.0
			O	4.6	5.2
		Males	Y	2.9	3.3
			O	5.3	5.2
	Middle Class	Females	Y	5.0	5.6
			O	4.1	5.2
		Males	Y	2.9	4.3
			O	3.0	3.5
WHITES	Hardcore	Females	Y	5.3	6.0
			O	7.2	7.2
		Males	Y	2.5	2.2
			O	5.6	5.8
	Working Class	Females	Y	7.0	7.0
			O	7.0	6.2
		Males	Y	5.9	5.5
			O	6.3	6.0
	Middle Class	Females	Y	5.6	6.3
			O	6.5	6.5
		Males	Y	3.3	3.9
			O	6.7	6.9

Table 2 Respect for Foremen and Policemen

				Black Job Foreman	Black Police-man	White Job Foreman	White Police-man
BLACKS	Hardcore	Females	Y	5.2	6.1	5.2	5.4
			O	6.0	6.5	5.4	6.5
		Males	Y	5.5	4.1	5.3	3.8
			O	4.8	7.0	4.8	6.8
	Working Class	Females	Y	5.2	5.9	5.3	6.5
			O	5.1	5.5	5.1	5.5
		Males	Y	5.8	5.3	4.0	3.7
			O	7.5	7.2	7.5	6.9
	Middle Class	Females	Y	4.6	6.1	4.9	5.0
			O	6.5	6.1	3.9	4.1
		Males	Y	7.0	4.9	4.4	3.8
			O	6.0	5.0	4.4	4.2
WHITES	Hardcore	Females	Y	5.2	5.9	5.0	5.7
			O	5.8	7.6	5.9	7.6
		Males	Y	4.7	3.7	5.1	4.5
			O	6.1	7.0	5.6	6.3
	Working Class	Females	Y	6.4	6.8	6.4	7.2
			O	5.9	7.8	5.8	7.8
		Males	Y	5.6	5.5	5.3	5.5
			O	5.3	6.7	5.6	6.6
	Middle Class	Females	Y	5.8	6.5	5.7	5.6
			O	5.3	6.8	5.3	6.6
		Males	Y	4.8	3.6	4.5	3.1
			O	6.3	6.5	6.6	6.3
Black*	Hardcore Males			5.0	4.7	5.2	3.6
	High School Males			4.2	3.9	4.6	2.8
White*	High School Males			3.7	4.8	4.4	5.4
	College Females			5.7	6.1	5.8	5.5

* Data from Triandis, Feldman, and Harvey, 1970.

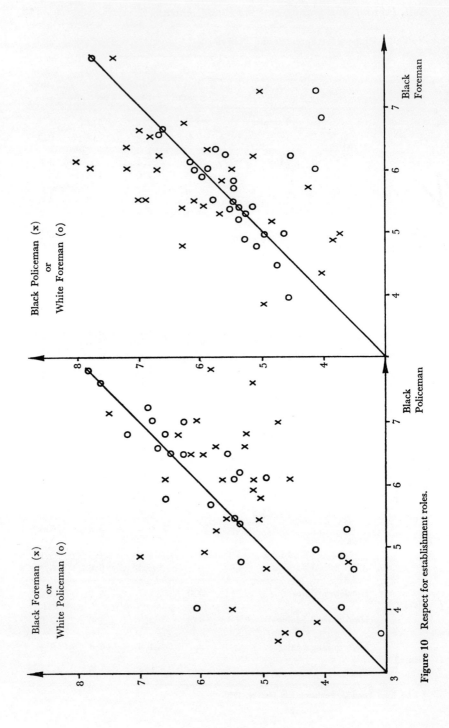

Figure 10   Respect for establishment roles.

The perception of interracial conflict roles is reflected in Figure 11. One strong finding is the great similarity between the samples in the perceptions of these roles. All perceive, for example, that a white policeman is more likely to *fight with, hit, discipline,* and *give orders to* a black demonstrator than a black militant is likely to do with a white man.

Only on three behaviors are the responses different. It appears that the black hardcore samples see the white policeman as much more likely to *play games with* a black demonstrator than is the case with

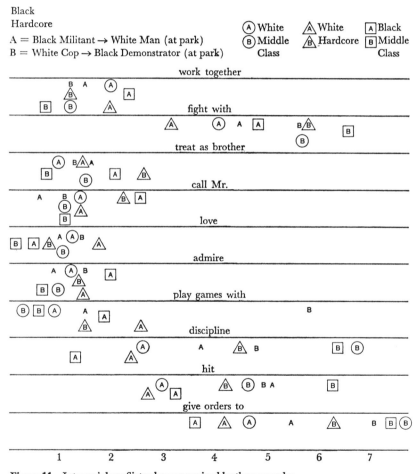

Figure 11 Interracial conflict roles as perceived by three samples.

the other samples. The middle class differentiate the white-to-black roles from the black-to-white roles on the *discipline* dimension to a greater extent than the hardcore, suggesting that they see the white policeman as "legitimate" much more than do the other samples; the same trend occurs on the scale *give orders to*.

Finally, there is a good deal of rejection among blacks of those who do well under the status quo. This is seen in subtle ways, in reactions to black professionals and black members of the establishment (policemen, foremen), but even more clearly in reactions to Uncle Toms and hustlers. These are more distrusted and there is a greater tendency to stay away from them among the black than among the white samples. Conversely, black militants receive more trust, respect, and tendency toward help from black than from white samples.

SUMMARY

In this chapter we examined the self-perceptions of the black hardcore, which we found to be appropriate reactions to a difficult environment. We then noted perceptions toward ingroups, in which we found among the hardcore a certain form of informality which generalized to work roles. Finally, there was considerable rejection of establishment roles and people who do well under the status quo among most black samples.

CHAPTER EIGHT

Perceptual Variations in Real-Life Interaction: Some Selected Examples

J. FELDMAN

Reading a book such as this, it is easy to become very abstract in one's conception of interpersonal processes. Yet if the data we have presented are to be meaningful and useful to the nonprofessional, abstractions must somehow be related to everyday experience. The culture assimilator attempts to do this in a teaching framework, as seen earlier. Since the incidents are for the most part taken from real-life experiences of black and white people, they can serve another function as well. In this chapter we will present incidents from the assimilator which will illustrate and provide concrete examples for the abstractions discussed in preceding chapters. These incidents are not scientific data in and of themselves — rather, they are intended to illustrate the effect of such factors as eco-system distrust on the relationships between black and white people. It is hoped that these incidents will give the reader an intuitive "feel" for the problems of intercultural relationships which the discussion of variables in abstract terms might not.

ASPECTS OF ECO-SYSTEM DISTRUST

CAUTION

We have said that eco-system distrust is a pervasive phenomenon in disadvantaged groups, caused by a lack of access to resources and resulting in intense competition and a perception of the world in zero-sum terms. The following incident will illustrate some of the interpersonal consequences of such distrust in a heterocultural setting.

241-1

About three months ago the company where Jim works instituted a program to seek black employees for the firm at all levels in the company hierarchy. Jim, a black electronics technician, was hired under this program as a specialist in circuit board design. For the past three weeks he has been working with Dave, another black employee, who has been with the company for two years. During the time they have worked together, they have become fairly close friends and partners in their work relationship.

One morning as they were changing from street clothes into their lab uniforms in the locker room, Jim said to Dave, "Hey man, I think I've finally debugged that circuit we were having problems with all week. I worked on it for four hours last night and I think I've finally got the answer."

"Jim, that's great!" Dave exclaimed with a happy grin, "If you're right, it'll really make our day. You might even get a raise out of this."

Talking excitedly about the design change, Jim and Dave continued to change their clothes. Just before they were finished changing, Jim interrupted Dave and said, "Hold on a minute, Dave. I've got to run to the john." Carefully, Jim locked his locker and tested the lock several times.

Puzzled, Dave said, "You don't have to do that, Jim, nobody is going to steal your things."

Jim replied, "Man, I don't trust anybody!" checking the lock one more time.

After Jim left, Pete, a white friend of Jim's who had been changing clothes a few lockers down, came over to Dave and asked, "Dave, why do you suppose he said that? I thought he was your friend."

Dave just smiled and replied, "He is."

As you can see, Jim's behavior seemed strange to Pete. One might even argue that Jim's behavior was inappropriate in the work environment. This argument ignores the powerful influence that habits of thought and behavior have in determining our actions. Long exposure to an environment where trust is often punished (as by the theft of property) can engender habits which require years to change. In any case, understanding Jim's behavior should prevent his co-workers from feeling that his distrust is aimed at them personally.

FORMALITY

Another aspect of eco-system distrust is a preference for formal relationships. This may exist because of the tendency of confidence men to use friendship as a means of gaining advantage over others, or because friendly behavior implies mutual obligation beyond formal work requirements. Whatever the reason, it is important to remember that formal speech does not necessarily imply disliking or social distance. In fact, it may indicate respect and liking in some contexts.

205-1

Several hardcore unemployed blacks had been hired by Jones Tool and Die Company. Mac Grove was one of the foremen who was supposed to train the blacks in the procedures of their new jobs. After he had explained the use of one machine, he asked, "Are there any questions?" One of the blacks replied, "Yes, Mr. Grove...." Mac interrupted, saying, "Oh, call me Mac. Everybody does."

The group moved on to another machine, and Mac explained its function. He was surprised when one of the blacks again addressed him as "Mr. Grove." He decided not to say anything, but he wondered if the men didn't like him.

SUSPICION

The following incident deals with the suspicion that can greet the most well-intentioned behavior. Since the scarcity of resources in ghetto neighborhoods makes truly altruistic behavior quite rare, suspicion such as that illustrated here should not be regarded as unusual or pathological.

524-1

Jill, a white college student, was working on a state-funded project channeling black seniors from disadvantaged areas into state universities and colleges. Her primary job was to help students assigned to her to get financial aid. Things seemed to be going well until one night when Jill received a phone call from one of the students. He and two friends asked her, "Exactly what kick-back do you get from this?"

DISTRUST OF AUTHORITY

It is common knowledge that poor black people often have bad experiences with police and other representatives of the establishment. It should not be surprising to learn that the distrust fostered by ghetto conditions may generalize to all authorities, whether black or white.

427-1

Jack, a white worker, and Sam, a black worker, left the factory where they both worked and walked toward home together. After they had walked a block or so, a squad car with two white policemen in it passed them. A block or so later another squad car with two black policemen came from the opposite direction. Sam made a rude gesture and said, "The pigs are everywhere today." Jack replied, surprised, "But they are black cops; doesn't that make a difference?"

Sam said shortly, "All cops are bad."

Jack went on home still wondering why Sam felt this way.

Another incident illustrates the same phenomenon in a different context. Here the authority figure occupies a role designed to help the workers, but the image of a man "making it in the system" prevents his immediate acceptance.

428-1

The Franklin Manufacturing Company employed a large number of workers, both black and white. Problems often arose between blacks and whites. The company encouraged the workers to see the personnel counselor, but almost none of the blacks went to him. They didn't seem to trust him, and felt he would favor the company and the white workers. So they hired a black counselor to counsel the blacks. At the end of the first month the company manager was quite disappointed to find that not many more blacks had gone to the black counselor than to the white. When the manager questioned a group of blacks about why they didn't like the black counselor, the blacks replied, "Oh, we like him well enough. In fact, we all had dinner at his house last week." This confused the manager even more.

CAUSE-EFFECT RELATIONSHIPS

People from ghetto areas are exposed to an environment that is less regular and predictable than that of the middle class. They learn that promises are often unkept, especially when made by organizations, and that things often fail to work out as expected. Thus one cannot expect the hardcore unemployed black to exert a great deal of effort on, or place his hopes in, a program that does not have clear and definite outcomes.

Some VISTA volunteers were working with southern black migrants in a large city. The volunteers were tutoring the blacks to prepare them for job training programs. The black trainees were very often late but never explained their lateness. The VISTA volunteers felt they were not late for any important reason, and that they had just been "messing around" in town. This irritated the volunteers and made the tutoring sessions tense.

Sources of Eco-system Distrust

We have spoken of the ghetto environment as the source of the distrust found to characterize many poor black people's views of the world. The following comments and incidents will graphically illustrate what this environment means to the people involved, and how generalized distrust becomes an adaptive response to such an environment. The incidents were told to our staff by particular blacks. The first is from a young black housewife.

A dry goods store was having a sale. I called before going there and the man told me the price of the lamp was $39.95. When I got to the store, there were two white people in the store who were buying a table and chair on sale. When the clerk came around to wait on me, he said the lamp that I wanted went up to $49.95. I asked him why. He said to go to the manager. The manager came over to talk to me and said, "That's just the way it is." So I asked him why he had let the lady and her husband have a table and chair and told them they were still on sale, but I could not get that lamp on sale for the same price. I believe he wanted more money out of me because I was black. I threatened to go to the store manager and he let me have the lamp.

A young black man's experience:

One particular time I was in a huge shopping center. I was wearing a big leather coat and a black hat. I had my hands in my pockets looking at some comic books. I wasn't really noticing anybody coming by. A white man in a white uniform came up to me. He was accompanied by two others. They told me to clear all my pockets, that the police were coming. One of them said I had stolen an item from the back of the shopping center. I was surprised that these whites had come up to me in that manner and told me to clear my pockets. They were surprised that

I laughed. When the police came the situation was cleared up, but I had to spend 3 or 4 hours in jail.

Blacks report job problems:

I had been working in the factory for 15 years. I was finally up for a promotion to supervisor. But a white got the position. I complained and the company agreed to work out a solution. They came back and said they were transferring the white guy to a different department and I could now have the position. When I reported to work that Monday, the manager asked me to meet him in his office. Due to "unforeseen circumstances" the department I was supposed to supervise had been closed out.

I finally saved up enough money to take the training program at the vocational school. I worked hard for six months and felt I was ready to get a good job. After six weeks of pounding the pavement, I took a job as a cleanup man. Most of the whites in the class seemed to have found jobs okay.

I was employed as a janitor for 20 years. When the white supervisor retired, I was promoted to that position. I was real proud and felt I had finally achieved something. But I ended up just training a younger white to take over the job.

511-1

Dave Wilson, a 24-year-old black man, has recently been working as a sales representative for a car lot. Occasionally, when a prospect is interested solely in a specific car, Dave has gone to see the person where he lives rather than having him come all the way to the lot.

Early one afternoon he drove over to see a customer, another black man. While Dave was showing him the car, a policeman came up to them. The cop pointed out that the car was in a "no parking" zone and told Dave to move it.

After Dave had moved it around the corner and started talking to his customer again, he noticed that the cop had followed them and was now looking kind of suspiciously at the dealer's license plates on the car. Deciding that it would be best to prove once and for all that he was a legitimate salesman, Dave went up to the cop and showed him his identification.

Shortly after the policeman had left, Dave started back to the car lot with the customer's car, in order to have it appraised. But he got back to the dealer's only to find out that his customer had meanwhile been arrested on suspicion of car theft.

ASPECTS OF SELF- AND OTHER-PERCEPTION

PERCEPTION OF AUTHORITY FIGURES

In Chapter 7 it was pointed out that hardcore unemployed blacks often see the "pose" as an important aspect of social life and as a requirement for getting ahead. This implies that non-hardcore people who behave in ways which are natural to them may be perceived as posing, especially when these people are also black. The following incidents will illustrate two sources of interpersonal difficulty stemming from this process. The first deals with foreman-worker relations, the second with relations between foremen.

426-1

George, a white worker, was talking to Joe, a fellow black worker, about the new black supervisor. Both Joe and George were "hardcore" unemployed. They had become friends while working on the job for a few days.

George, the white worker, was saying, "Man, I really dig that black supervisor. He seems so intelligent. Did you notice how smoothly he spoke to us?"

At this time Joe said angrily, "Man, I just can't relate to that dude. Why he talk so proper? If I wasn't lookin' at him, I wouldn't even know he was a brother."

423-1

Joe, a white supervisor, was a very good friend of John, a black supervisor. However, Joe noticed that John talked quite differently from his white friends. Joe usually understood what John was saying, but it troubled him that John spoke differently. He was also surprised since John had received his M.A. degree at a major university.

Well, one day in a conversation John used the word "walkin'" instead of "walking." This was Joe's chance. He asked John, "Why do you use improper English if you have a college degree?" John became angry and said, "Because I went to college don't mean I have to talk like white folks. Besides, you understood what I meant, didn't you?" Joe said, "Yes," but couldn't understand John's anger.

MATERNAL RESPECT

We have stressed the respect and reverence in which many black people hold the concept "mother." The following incident brings home this point very strongly.

412-1

A minor dispute arose in a factory between Dave, a white, and Frank, a black, over the ownership of a tool. During the verbal exchange both workers called each other names, but the tone of the dispute was not particularly hostile. They were merely wrangling rather good-naturedly over who owned the tool. However, when Dave said, "You son of a bitch, don't you even know what tools you own?" Frank became outraged and hit Dave.

Ingroup Behavior

The next incident points out quite clearly that behavior which is permitted and encouraged among ingroup members is often viewed negatively when done by an outsider. It is important to remember that this principle holds for all people, not just blacks.

420-1

John Howard is 19 years old and white. When he graduated from high school about a year before, he decided that he should move away from home. After settling into a small place of his own, he began working at an automobile factory, where he is still employed.

Several of his co-workers at the factory are black. Since he grew up in a small city that was predominantly white, this is almost the only contact that he has ever had with black people. He finds himself quite surprised by much of the joking that he hears them doing among themselves, by the way that they talk to one another.

At lunch one day he goes up to his foreman and says, "Can I ask you something?"

"Sure," the foreman says.

"It's about these Negroes that work here."

"You having a problem with one of them?" the foreman quickly asks.

"Oh, no," John replies. "Nothing like that. It's about something I've heard them saying to each other." He pauses for a moment. "How come they call each other nigger when they talk to each other? I thought they didn't like that, and they'd never let one of us call them that. But they do all the time."

"Beats me," the foreman says, shrugging his shoulders. "They are kind of strange in a lot of ways."

INGROUP INFORMALITY

We have seen data suggesting that hardcore unemployed people expect less formality in ingroup roles, including less giving and taking of orders. It also appears that foreman-worker relationships take on some of the aspects of ingroup roles. This should be especially true where a friendship exists between a foreman and a worker. However, this situation may result in some interpersonal difficulties, as illustrated by the following incident.

236-1

Gene was a white foreman in a small shop. He supervised twelve employees, most of whom were also white. However, there was one black employee, Harold, with whom he had become especially friendly since Harold began working at the shop six months earlier. They bowled together on Wednesday nights and often went for beers together after work. They also usually ate lunch together. Gene, though, began to notice that although Harold was a hard worker, at times it was quite difficult to get him to perform certain duties around the shop — especially those tasks which he knew Harold disliked. It seemed that the friendlier they became, the less Harold wanted to follow his orders.

The greater informality of the work situation, as perceived by the black hardcore, can often result in misunderstandings and feelings of unfair treatment. In the next incident, for example, there is no suggestion that the black worker was lazy or irresponsible. Rather, he perceived the job in a less formal way than his white foreman and co-workers did.

106-1

Bob Lewis, a 24-year-old black man, has just completed a training program for the hardcore unemployed at an aircraft company. He has been assigned to the painting division. His third morning on the job, the foreman, Ed Michaels, assigns Bob to work on painting a section of the hanger with three white painters.

Dividing the wall space to be painted into about four equal sections, Ed tells all the men that it should take about four hours for each man to finish his section and that he will return at about noon. He further instructs them that if there are any problems or if they need him for anything, he will be in his office.

Bob immediately sets to painting his area very rapidly. By 11:15 he has finished; he cleans his brush and sits down in a corner. Since each of the other painters is only about three-quarters done, they all ask Bob for help. Just ignoring them, he falls asleep.

When the foreman returns at 11:40, he sees Bob asleep and the others still working. "Bob, wake up!" Ed shouts, shaking Bob. "What the hell do you think you're doing sleeping on the job? If anybody saw you sleeping there, I'd be in big trouble. What the hell is wrong with you, anyway?"

"Why are you yelling at me?" Bob asks. "My work is done. You should be hassling those other dudes; they aren't even finished yet. I'm the best worker you got." Bob is quite angry at the foreman.

EXPECTATION OF RESPECT

One important aspect of ingroup relationships is that the members treat one another with a greater degree of mutual respect and consideration. Thus black workers expect respectful treatment from foremen rather than authoritarian behavior. A lack of such respect and consideration is likely to result in an incident such as the following.

233-1

Fred, a young black high school dropout, had just been hired as a worker on a loading dock. This was his first job. Joe, a young white, was hired the same day. Not knowing quite what to do on the first day, they sat down after they had finished their first job assignment. Finally, the white foreman noticed they weren't doing anything and came and said, "Get off your lazy asses and go help unload that truck."

Joe got up and started to work while Fred walked away muttering angrily, "Who does he think he is, talking to us that way. I never expected to be treated like *this* on a job." After that one day Fred never returned to the job.

CYNICISM

We have said that the black hardcore are often cynical about their chances of getting ahead in organizations. They may believe that good relationships and advancement are unrelated to job performance, and that ingratiation is a prerequisite for success on the job.

127-1

Jay, an employment counselor, was showing an older black man, Walter, a list of unskilled and semi-skilled jobs for which he would qualify. Included on the list were jobs as dishwashers, hotel bellhops, gardeners, semi-skilled construction workers, etc. Jay was trying to find out what Walter preferred to do.

He asked, "Would you rather work indoors or outdoors?"

Walter replied, "Don't make no difference."

Jay pursued, "Do you prefer to work with others or by yourself?"

Again Walter replied, "Don't matter one way or the other."

"It seems to me you don't care what you do," Jay said.

Walter responded, "I don't. One job is as bad as another. I just got to make some money for my family."

FINAL NOTE

It should be remembered that any single incident can be explained in a number of ways, some of which are inconsistent with the principles presented here. The principles are useful in that they allow a number of seemingly different behaviors to be understood as ramifications of a single underlying concept. If one's own experience and observations suggest different explanatory principles, some thought might allow him to reconcile his theory of interracial behavior with that presented here. It may also be that our investigations have missed some phenomena. In any case, there is no substitute for continually testing any set of generalizations against systematic observations of the world. We have attempted to provide a framework for such observations, but, like any tool, it should be replaced when the situation dictates a new approach. It is hoped that the present chapter has illustrated the application of theoretical principles and generalizations, preparing the way for a more systematic and thorough observation of the world on the part of the reader.

CHAPTER NINE

Summary and Implications

H. C. TRIANDIS AND W. HARVEY

FINDINGS

The major findings reported in the earlier chapters of this book are as follows.

1. There is a general "eco-system distrust" among blacks, particularly the black hardcore. This is reflected in not trusting people, not trusting themselves, not trusting the way establishment institutions function, and not trusting the dependability of relationships between events occurring in their environment.

2. The black hardcore react to themselves with a good deal of ambivalence. They do not think of themselves as being as important, as do other samples; they seem to value power more than they value "being nice," while the reverse is true for the middle class.

3. The black hardcore see social relations as involving a "pose" in which one tries to appear better than he really is, while the middle class emphasize "openness" and being nice. However, it appears that the black hardcore posture is functional for adjustment under the conditions of the ghetto. Thus it can be considered a "healthy" response to an "unhealthy" environment.

4. The ghetto blacks accept conditions in the ghetto to a much greater extent than do other samples. This is again seen as a positive factor in their adjustment.

5. The black samples see ingroup relations as more matrifocal.

6. The black hardcore see ingroup relations as more informal.

7. All black samples and the white hardcore use the scale *call him Mr.* (*her Mrs.*) to reflect both positive affect and formality, with much more weight given to affect than to formality.

8. Black ghetto samples see work relations as more informal than other samples.

9. Both race groups see actors of their own race as less prejudiced than actors of the other race.

10. Black hardcore samples see a white foreman as more likely to show favoritism to white workers than do other samples.

11. Blacks, and all hardcore samples, see work roles as similar to family roles.

12. Hardcore blacks have a more cynical view of work relations with supervisors than do other samples.

13. Blacks and hardcore samples reject establishment roles, such as black or white policemen, ministers, and foremen, more than do whites or the middle class. The black hardcore see black professionals as self-serving, intelligent egotists.

14. All samples react to whites and blacks who are in establishment roles according to the role, not the race.

15. Middle-class samples, both white and black, see greater legitimacy than other samples in establishment roles.

16. Whites accept people who do well under the status quo (e.g., Uncle Toms) much more than do blacks.

17. Blacks accept black militants much more than do whites.

The broad set of findings is sufficiently consistent with reviews of the literature concerning the effects of poverty that we feel relatively confident that we have tapped reliable phenomena. For example, Bruner (1971), after a review of the effects of poverty, concludes: "Persistent poverty over generations creates a culture of survival. Goals are short range and restricted. The outsider and the outside are suspect. One stays inside and gets what one can. Beating the system takes the place of using the system" (p. 160). This is not far from our definition of eco-system distrust.

These findings must be viewed within the context of some generalizations that are even more important.

1. There are more similarities than differences in the responses of blacks and whites.

2. There is tremendous heterogeneity in the responses of both blacks and whites. Specifically, there are several black points of view. For example, some blacks are much more like the white middle class than

they are like other blacks. The hardcore blacks are the only black sample that is consistently most different from the white middle class.

3. There is symmetry in interracial conflict. Both groups perceive it about equally. However, there is a tendency for blacks to admit more hostility toward white men than the other way around; women do not receive the same degree of black rejection.

INTERPRETATION

A special study group appointed by the National Institutes of Health was critical of the way problem research is being conducted in the United States. A summary of this report (see *Behavior Today,* 4 [Apr. 23, 1973]:2) states that the major complaint was that studies do not make appropriate analyses of the psychological impact of social structure. The argument goes that there are common causes to a variety of social problems — crime, drug addiction, etc. — which are overlooked by researchers when they focus on specific causes of each problem.

The report suggests that a broad cause affecting many problems is the social structure and ethnicity of the group. The report advocates greater research efforts in the direction of discovering the relationship between social structure and psychological functioning. The argument is justified by the following points: (1) Social structure is a more important variable than those that are typically studied. (2) Such studies will clarify how particular policy changes will affect different social groups. (3) We might be able to intervene more directly in the case of social structural variables. (4) This kind of study can lead to better understanding of how psychological processes both are affected by and influence social structure.

The present report is an effort in that direction. It does consider social class, together with ethnicity, sex, and age, as important correlates of the way a person looks at his social environment, and tries to describe variations in such points of view. The data should be interpreted within such a framework.

Social class and ethnicity affect both whites and blacks, thus creating the heterogeneity stressed above. But the black ghetto provides an unusual environment. On the one hand, it is located in the middle of affluent cities, with access to cultural models of well-to-do heroes and heroines. On the other hand, it is located on an extreme point of deprivation and exploitation on the economic scale. When the pressure-cooker effects of lack of opportunity for advancement through established institutions (e.g., schools), of housing discrimination, and of confrontations with exploitative landlords, loan sharks, and a biased legal system are added to repeated experiences of failure, the result is an unusual perception of the social environment.

One way to summarize these perceptions of the social environment is to use the term "eco-system distrust." A case can be made that eco-system distrust is functional in the ghetto. However, a case can also be made that eco-system distrust is not functional in a modern industrial environment. An important aspect of modern industrial environments is that they are large-scale and assume that people will cooperate, conform to the norms of the group, and adjust to the rules set up by the leadership of the institutions. A person with high eco-system distrust is particularly unlikely to be a good "organization man." Furthermore, such highly bureaucratic institutions are not geared for people with low self-esteem, since they are unable to deal with individual cases, to counsel and support, and help the individual with a low self-esteem. The result is that a low self-esteem person is likely to find such environments very punishing and to leave them. In short, the economic and social conditions of the ghetto create psychological conditions which make adjustment to industrial or to middle-class environments extremely difficult, if not impossible.

The concept of eco-system distrust seems to be useful. It suggests a focus for efforts to integrate blacks with this point of view into a society which requires trust. One must convince blacks with such points of view that the system can be trusted, that people can be trusted, and that phenomena in their environment are related to each other in lawful ways. This can probably be done most successfully if the environment *is* made more reliable. However, it also requires much effort on the part of whites to disconfirm this point of view. For example, a white foreman who knows that his black workers will assume that he is prejudiced whenever he gives them the slightest opportunity to think so (even if he does not have a trace of prejudice) is warned about the importance of *explaining* his behavior. He simply cannot assume that his behavior will be given the benefit of the doubt.

Every human behavior can be misinterpreted. Even the most positive behaviors can be seen as "ingratiation," "conforming to government regulations," or "being nice to catch me off guard." Thus the foreman whose employees are characterized by eco-system distrust has a major problem on his hands. He has to learn the symbols of "correct" interracial behavior. Such behavior must emphasize interpersonal respect (e.g., he may have to call his employees Mr. and Mrs., while at the same time acting toward them with greater intimacy than implied by such forms of address). He may have to learn the concept of "reparation" for past injustices. He will without doubt have to learn more about communication. To reduce barriers of meaningful discussion between foreman and worker, he will have to learn to appreciate the viewpoint of the black hardcore worker, and reduce the defensiveness that such a worker is likely to experience about his own behavior. As the worker is helped to think about his own behavior and its consequences (e.g., absenteeism, lateness), the behavior will begin to be "shaped" and come under the "control" of the worker. Making the worker defensive is a guarantee that he will not change his behavior. In short, foremen need to learn to be counselors.

Another theme that emerged from our data is the black ghetto sample's high valuation of "power" rather than "niceness." This will normally not produce problems when a supervisor has much power, but it can create difficulties when he has little power. Furthermore, it can be a problem for the relationships between a black worker and his fellow workers who do not have this orientation. Given the heterogeneity of the blacks, one should probably not try to design training programs to counteract this tendency, but one should simply inform the foremen that this is a potential problem which requires sensitivity to the possible implications of their behavior to their workers. Incidentally, foremen who consider the implications of their behavior, as perceived by their workers, will probably show a general improvement in their social relations.

There are numerous findings concerning the reactions of the samples to situations that occur frequently in the ghetto — getting robbed, stealing, using drugs, etc. Generally, there is less expressed concern for these events among the black hardcore. They also do not get particularly excited about them. A "level of adaptation" interpretation of this observation seems most reasonable. People conceive of events as "normal" by taking into account their past experiences with such events. When an event occurs frequently, the level of "perceived normality" goes up. For example, if there are two robberies a night in a neighborhood, this level will be perceived as normal over a period of time. Then one robbery per night will appear as a rate so low as to be insignificant. In an environment with one robbery per month, one robbery per day will appear extremely high.

A most interesting difference was obtained in reactions of the samples to TO DO YOUR OWN THING. The blacks and the hardcore samples seem to think that one consequence will be *get into trouble*. The middle class see self-improvement and self-actualization themes connected with this concept. Our interpretation is that the environment of the middle class is designed by the middle class for the middle class; if they do their own thing, it is good for them. The environment of the ghetto is a consequence of exploitative economic conditions. It is not designed by the ghetto dwellers and it is not good for anybody. Doing your own thing in that environment leads to trouble.

The finding that *call him Mr.* implies positive affect for blacks suggests that whites should be trained to use this form of address to a greater extent than they are currently likely to do. However, this does *not* mean that they should create formality in work relations. On the contrary, blacks prefer informality. The problem is to establish work relations that are as informal as is practical, given the constraints of technology. Given that large size and technology may require more formal relations, blacks have to be trained to differentiate work and ingroup situations along the formality dimension. At the same time, foremen must be instructed that some black workers may have a more cynical view of relations with them than they are used to. Again, sensitivity to this possibility may serve a foreman well.

The greater legitimacy of establishment roles for the whites than for the blacks is another area which might require training in both directions. Whites might be taught the black's perceptions and given an explanation, such as that some blacks have had many experiences in which establishment institutions have discriminated against them and they naturally developed this viewpoint. The blacks might be given some insight into the meaning of such differences, particularly as they are likely to lead to unfortunate encounters with the legal system. A training program that rewards blacks for participation in the establishment (e.g., rewarding coming on time, accepting foreman's orders, etc.) might be helpful. Here we have a situation in which one might reward behaviors which are usually not rewarded. The rationale is simple: mainstream people get rewarded for reacting appropriately to the establishment when they are very young. Blacks from the ghetto may miss this form of socialization, which can only be "made up" by providing these rewarding experiences later in life.

SPECULATIVE IMPLICATIONS

What do these data imply, if anything, for the great issues of the day — integration, bussing, law and order, inflation, unemployment? The discussion that follows is speculative but, we hope, well reasoned.

First, consider the implications of the very considerable heterogeneity of both the blacks and the whites. Social policy has usually dealt with broad categories — blacks, unemployed, etc. However, is this reasonable when there is so much heterogeneity?

On the issue of integration and its correlates, such as bussing, it may be necessary to increase the distinctions concerning who is to be integrated, when. While undoubtedly integration will be the long-run answer, the time, place, and manner of integration may be handled differently depending on whether we take the facts of heterogeneity seriously. The majority of blacks studied appear to be similar enough to whites that the time is *now*. But there are blacks who are very different from other black samples, let alone whites. There are reasons to believe that integrating these particular blacks now might produce more problems than it would solve.

It should also be made clear that many black leaders have lost their enthusiasm for integration. They argue that they see no sense in integrating into a "sick system." Some of the changes that we suggest later in this chapter will hopefully improve "the system" so that the black leadership will once again see more hope in the concept of integration.

To take this issue out of the present context, with its emotional connotations, let us see what happens when two groups of people come in contact. Triandis and Vassiliou (1967) studied this phenomenon with samples of Greeks and Americans having different amounts of actual contact. Vassiliou et al. (1972) studied it in great detail for representative samples of Greeks having different amounts of reported contact with Americans and large samples of Americans having contact with Greeks. The two studies gave results that were quite consistent. Specifically, the greater the amount of contact between Americans and Greeks, the more *negative* was the stereotype of Greeks given by Americans. The theoretical analysis which generated the study and which was supported by the data argued that when two groups have unequal standards of living, contact can have negative consequences. The details will not be discussed here, but the essential point is that differences in the standard of living are associated with numerous "evaluative" judgments. Somehow one has to "explain" to himself why he is richer than the other person. The tendency is to create cognitive consistency by thinking "I am better" than the other person; hence the other group is less "good." Triandis and Vassiliou found, consistent with this argument, that the way Americans looked at themselves *improved* with contact with Greeks, while at the same time their stereotypes of Greeks deteriorated in a number of ways, although not on all traits. A detailed look at the changes of the stereotype with contact showed that contact makes the stereotype more "realistic," but also that the difference in the position of the two groups on any trait is the determinant of how much each group is stereotyped. For example, if group A is clean and group B is *very* clean, group B will stereotype A as dirty even though on objective grounds both are clean.

The lesson to be derived from these studies is that contact is not necessarily beneficial. This is a point that is also made by Taylor (1974) after a careful review of the issues of integration. Taylor argues that the first thing that must be accomplished is to equalize power. Blacks and whites should have similar amounts of power. Only then is contact likely to lead to improvements in interpersonal relationships. Triandis and Vassiliou would argue that equality must be achieved not only in terms of power, although that is very important, but on *any* valued trait. If unequally distributed, any valued trait will reduce the likelihood that contact will lead to positive interpersonal experiences. We need to have similarity in valued traits first; then contact is likely to lead to good relations.

Returning to the implications of heterogeneity, we can see that it implies very strongly that a uniform policy dealing with "all blacks" would be counterproductive. One that deals with "most blacks" is much more likely to lead to positive interpersonal experiences. In short, the black middle and working classes should be integrated as fast as possible. But the black hardcore require a special set of policies.

They need to be "hooked" into the economic system and taught how to derive satisfactions from the system. This requires extensive training, not only of the black hardcore but also of those who will work with them. We have developed programs to train these blacks to understand the middle-class point of view and to train whites to understand the hardcore. Such programs *may* offer the hope that eventually the hardcore can be incorporated into the economic life of the country. Such incorporation, however, also requires extensive counseling, support when facing the exploitative institutions surrounding the black ghetto, and training of those who come in contact with the black hardcore. An extended discussion of these problems can be found in Fromkin and Sherwood (1974).

In all probability this will require a generation of black professionals who will devote their talents to the problem. Above all, it should be clear that the solution is to seek not the "rehabilitation" of the black hardcore but the modification of the system of influences which put them in their present position. If that exploitative system is not changed, the ghettoes will continue to produce a regular "output" of black hardcore who will need "rehabilitation." In short, "rehabilitation" means treating the symptoms, not the causes. This is not to say that we should not rehabilitate; that is the humane thing to do. But we must not put our major resources there. Nor should we expect complete integration in less than a generation.

To summarize, then, we believe that our data imply moves toward speedy integration for the majority of blacks, but careful and more expensive moves toward integration for other black samples.

We must recognize that some black people belong to a very different culture and cannot be integrated into the mainstream without extensive training and major modifications in the structure of the system that created them. We need vigorous programs to reduce unemployment and bring most of these people into the economic system. We need to commit resources for counseling, for assistance, and some for "rehabilitation."

The law-and-order issue is also related to the direction of solution of these problems. We are dealing with subcultures in which extralegal activities are rewarded and other "normal" activities are not. It is only when we restructure the system to give many rewards for behavior consistent with productive work that we are likely to obtain significant changes in behavior. The present system is designed for a maximum increase in the rate of crime. First, young people are made envious of all the "good things" they see around them which are not accessible, except extralegally. Their normal advancement is blocked because the educational system and other systems with which they are confronted hinder their progress. Under such conditions any human is likely to run afoul of the law. As soon as this happens, he is placed in an environment where hardened criminals teach him the tricks of their trade and where he acquires norms and roles that are incompatible with normal functioning in the mainstream.

The proposed programs suggested in this section will be expensive. It seems reasonable to think of one or two generations (30-40 years) of substantial expenditures to implement the programs. Such redirection of national effort requires a different perspective.

The effort is going to have to be even larger, because it is not possible, politically, to concentrate on only one ethnic group. Nor is it defensible morally. Thus, although the concept of "reparation" for years of previous exploitation may be viable, it must also be extended to those whites, American Indians, Chicanos, and others who for one reason or another have been exploited in the past. The record of dominant culture relationships with the Indians is particularly shocking.

We need to begin in our schools to teach how the environment shapes human behavior. The ghetto is an unusual environment. We must teach our children that any human who is forced to live there is likely to develop some of the characteristics of our hardcore sample. If they want to have an environment that is safe, cooperative, and where they and their children can grow to their full potential, they must help all others to do the same. We cannot have one way of life in one neighborhood and a completely different one in another. Most people will probably agree that a safe, cooperative, and equal-opportunity society is worth spending money for. Higher taxes may be necessary. Such taxes can provide good investments for a better future for our grandchildren.

At any rate, a substantial shift in priorities from military expenditures to purchase weapons that become obsolete every few years, requiring even larger expenditures, to (a) research which will keep us ready to produce the latest weapons and (b) investment in human resources, which is the essential ingredient of any military effort, seems to be appropriate. Finding a way to bring the standard of living of the poor to the level of the working class, for all ethnic groups, will require an enormous effort in the restructuring of economic opportunities and our educational system and the development of information programs for adults. If the society is to change fast enough to make it possible for those who are now poor to acquire a decent standard of living, within 20 years, it will be necessary to develop enormous political support for such redirection of effort. Such shifts in emphasis will require extensive programs of adult education — particularly education of parents about how to bring up their children — and information on "what leads to what." If enough people understand the implications of such redirection efforts for their own lives, there may develop enough support.

Our educational system needs to examine these problems in the light of both history and economics. It must help people understand how wage differentials work, how economic exploitation leads to "rationalizations" which justify it, how slavery resulted in particular institutions and folkways that continued the economic exploitation for generations, how these conditions led to major migrations which created the ghettoes, and how the latter supplied cheap labor when it was needed.

In this educational process, this present volume should have a place. It reflects, in quantitative terms, the subjective reactions of the black ghetto. It should help all those who read it, both black and white, develop a sense of "There but for the grace of God go I." As the reader looks at the cognitive maps of people living behind ghetto walls, he should realize that they are normal responses to an abnormal social environment, and he should try to support programs of action which will change that environment.

Appendix: Microfiche Tables

STEREOTYPES

BEHAVIORAL INTENTIONS

ROLE PERCEPTIONS

MF 213–214   Table 104 — Antecedents of TO USE DRUGS (ANY ILLEGAL DRUGS) (Phase II)

MF 215–216   Table 105 — Consequents of TO USE DRUGS (ANY ILLEGAL DRUGS) (Phase II)

MF 217–218   Table 106 — Antecedents of TO STEAL (Phase II)

MF 219–220   Table 107 — Consequents of TO STEAL (Phase II)

MF 221–222   Table 108 — Antecedents of TO NOT BE DEPENDENT ON OTHERS (Phase II)

MF 223–224   Table 109 — Consequents of TO NOT BE DEPENDENT ON OTHERS (Phase II)

CARD 3 — ROW C

MF 225–226   Table 110 — Antecedents of TO BE RESPECTED AND ADMIRED BY OTHERS (Phase II)

MF 227–228   Table 111 — Consequents of TO BE RESPECTED AND ADMIRED BY OTHERS (Phase II)

MF 229–230   Table 112 — Antecedents of TO HAVE GOOD FRIENDS (Phase II)

MF 231–232   Table 113 — Consequents of TO HAVE GOOD FRIENDS (Phase II)

MF 233–235   Table 114 — Antecedents of TO HAVE GOOD FRIENDS (Phase III)

MF 236–238   Table 115 — Consequents of TO HAVE GOOD FRIENDS (Phase III)

CARD 3 — ROW D

MF 239–240   Table 116 — Antecedents of TO HAVE DIGNITY (Phase II)

MF 241–242   Table 117 — Consequents of TO HAVE DIGNITY (Phase II)

MF 243–244   Table 118 — Antecedents of TO BUY A CAR (Phase II)

MF 245–246   Table 119 — Consequents of TO BUY A CAR (Phase II)

MF 247–248   Table 120 — Antecedents of TO DO YOUR OWN THING (Phase II)

MF 249–250   Table 121 — Antecedents of TO BUY FINE CLOTHES (Phase II)

MF 251–252   Table 122 — Consequents of TO BUY FINE CLOTHES (Phase II)

CARD 3 — ROW E

MF 253–254   Table 123 — Antecedents of TO GET A GIRLFRIEND (OR BOYFRIEND) (Phase II)

MF 255–256   Table 124 — Consequents of TO GET A GIRLFRIEND (OR BOYFRIEND) (Phase II)

MF 257–258   Table 125 — Antecedents of TO JOIN A MILITANT OR REVOLUTIONARY GROUP (Phase II)

References

Adams, J. S. 1965. Inequity in social exchange. In L. Berkowitz, ed., *Advances in experimental social psychology.* New York: Academic Press. Pp. 267-300.

Allport, F. H. 1955. *Theories of perception and the concept of structure.* New York: John Wiley.

Allport, G. W. 1954. *The nature of prejudice.* Reading, Mass.: Addison-Wesley.

Argyle, M., and Kendon, A. 1967. The experimental analysis of social performance. In L. Berkowitz, ed., *Advances in experimental social psychology.* New York: Academic Press. Pp. 55-98.

Avigdor, R. 1953. Études expérimentales de la genèse des stéréotypes. *Cahier International de Sociologie.* Pp. 154-168.

Ayrer, J. E., and Farber, I. J. 1972. The semantic structure of a set of scales developed for use with inner-city pupils. Paper presented at the American Educational Research Association, Chicago.

Banfield, E. C. 1958. *The moral basis of a backward society.* Glencoe, Ill.: Free Press.

Baratz, J. C. 1969. Teaching reading in an urban Negro school system. In J. C. Baratz and R. W. Shuy, eds., *Teaching black children to read.* Washington, D.C.: Center for Applied Linguistics. Pp. 92-116.

Baratz, L. S., and Baratz, J. C. 1970. Early childhood intervention: The social basis of institutional racism. *Harvard Educational Review,* 40: 29-50.

Baughman, E. E. 1971. *Black Americans: A psychological analysis.* New York: Academic Press.

Bear, G. 1973. Personal communication.

Bentler, P. M., and Lavoie, A. L. 1972. A nonverbal semantic differential. *Journal of Verbal Learning and Verbal Behavior,* 11: 491-496.

Biddle, B. J., and Thomas, E. J. 1966. *Role theory: Concepts and research.* New York: John Wiley.

Blumberg, L., and Winch, R. F. 1972. Societal complexity and familial complexity: Evidence for the curvilinear hypothesis. *American Journal of Sociology,* 77: 896-920.

Bobren, H.; Hill, C.; Snider, J.; and Osgood, C. 1969. A bibliography of literature relevant to the semantic differential technique. In J. G. Snider and C. E. Osgood, eds., *Semantic differential technique.* Chicago: Aldine-Atherton. Pp. 637-676.

Brislin, R. 1970. Personal communication.

Bruner, J. S. 1971. *The relevance of education.* New York: W. W. Norton.

Buchler, J. 1955. *Philosophical writings of Peirce.* New York: Dover.

Byrne, D. 1969. Attitudes and attraction. In L. Berkowitz, ed., *Advances in experimental social psychology.* New York: Academic Press. Pp. 36-90.

————. 1971. *The attraction paradigm.* New York: Academic Press.

Campbell, A. 1968. Civil rights and the vote for president. *Psychology Today,* 1: 26-70.

Campbell, D. T. 1967. Stereotypes and the perception of group differences. *American Psychologist,* 22: 817-829.

Clark, K. B. 1965. *Black ghetto: Dilemmas of social power.* New York: Harper.

Creelman, M. B. 1966. *The experimental investigation of meaning: A review of the literature.* New York: Springer.

Deutscher, I., and Thompson, E. J. 1968. *Among the people: Encounters with the poor.* New York: Basic Books.

Ehrlich, H. J. 1973. *The social psychology of prejudice.* New York: John Wiley.

Erskine, H. 1969. The polls: Negro philosophies of life. *Public Opinion Quarterly,* 33: 147-158.

Fanon, F. 1967. *Black skin, white masks.* New York: Grove Press.

Farber, R., and Schmeidler, G. 1971. Race differences in children's responses to "black" and "white." *Perceptual and Motor Skills,* 33: 359-363.

Ferman, L. A. 1968. *The Negro and equal employment opportunities.* New York: Frederick A. Praeger.

Fiedler, F. E.; Mitchell, T.; and Triandis, H. C. 1971. The culture assimilator: An approach to cross-cultural training. *Journal of Applied Psychology,* 55: 95-102.

Fishbein, M., and Ajzen, I. 1972. Attitudes and opinions. *Annual Review of Psychology.* Pp. 487-544.

————. 1973. Attribution of responsibility: A theoretical note. *Journal of Experimental Social Psychology,* 9: 148-153.

Flanagan, J. C. 1954. The critical incident technique. *Psychological Bulletin,* 51: 327-358.

Foa, U. G. 1971. Interpersonal and economic resources. *Science,* 171: 345-351.

Foa, U. G.; Triandis, H. C.; and Katz, E. W. 1966. Cross-cultural invariance in the differentiation and organization of family roles. *Journal of Personality and Social Psychology,* 4: 316-327.

Foster, G. M. 1965. Peasant society and the image of limited good. *American Anthropologist,* 67: 293-315.

Frazier, E. F. 1932. *The Negro family in Chicago.* Chicago: University of Chicago Press.

————. 1966. *The Negro family in the United States.* Rev. and abridged ed. Chicago: University of Chicago Press.

Fromkin, H. L., and Sherwood, J. J. 1974. *Integrating the organization: A social psychological analysis.* Glencoe, Ill.: Free Press.

Gibson, E. J. 1969. *Principles of perceptual learning and development.* New York: Appleton-Century-Crofts.

Gladwin, T. 1967. *Poverty U. S. A.* Boston: Little, Brown.

Glazer, N., and Moynihan, D. P. 1963. *Beyond the melting pot: The Negroes, Puerto Ricans, Jews, Italians, and Irish of New York City.* Cambridge, Mass.: M.I.T. Press and Harvard University Press.

Goldschmid, M. L. 1970. *Black Americans and white racism: Theory and research.* New York: Holt, Rinehart and Winston.

Goodale, J. G. 1973. Effects of personal background and training on work values of the hardcore unemployed. *Journal of Applied Psychology,* 57: 1-9.

Haley, A., and Malcolm X. 1964. *The autobiography of Malcolm X.* New York: Grove Press.

Hall, W. S., and Freedle, R. 1973. Notes. *Educational Testing Service Research Bulletin.* Pp. 8-10.

Hammond, K. R. 1966. *The psychology of Egon Brunswik.* New York: Holt, Rinehart and Winston.

Hannerz, U. 1969. *Soulside: Inquiries into ghetto culture and community.* New York: Columbia University Press.

Harman, H. 1968. *Modern factor analysis.* Chicago: University of Chicago Press.

Harris, C. W., and Kaiser, H. F. 1964. Oblique factor analytic solutions by orthogonal transformations. *Psychometrika,* 29: 347-362.

Hauser, S. T. 1971. *Black and white identity formation.* New York: John Wiley.

Heaps, R. A. 1972. Use of the semantic differential technique in research: Some precautions. *Journal of Psychology,* 80: 121-125.

Heise, D. R. 1969. Some methodological issues in semantic differential research. *Psychological Bulletin,* 72: 406-422.

Herskovits, M. J. 1955. *Cultural anthropology.* New York: Alfred A. Knopf.

Hess, R. D., and Shipman, O. C. 1965. Early experience and the socialization of cognitive modes in children. *Child Development,* 36: 869-886.

Hooper, P. P., and Powell, E. R. 1971. Note on oral comprehension in standard and non-standard English. *Perceptual and Motor Skills,* 33: 34.

Jacobs, P. 1966. *Prelude to riot: A view of urban America from the bottom.* New York: Random House.

Jenck, C. 1973. *Inequity: A reassessment of the effort of family and schooling in America.* New York: Harper and Row.

Jensen, A. R. 1969. How much can we boost IQ and scholastic achievement? *Harvard Educational Review,* 39: 1-123.

Jones, E. E., and Nisbett, R. E. 1971. *The actor and the observer: Divergent perceptions of the causes of behavior.* New York: General Learning Press.

————. 1972. The actor and the observer: Divergent perceptions of the causes of behavior. In E. E. Jones et al., eds., *Attribution: Perceiving the causes of behavior.* Morristown, N.J.: General Learning Press. Pp. 79-94.

Jones, R. L. 1972. *Black psychology.* New York: Harper and Row.

Keil, C. 1966. *Urban blues.* Chicago: University of Chicago Press.

Kochman, T. 1969. "Rapping" in the black ghetto. *Transaction,* 6: 29-34.

Komorita, S. S., and Bass, A. R. 1967. Attitude differentiation and evaluative scales of the semantic differential. *Journal of Personality and Social Psychology,* 6: 241-244.

Kuhn, T. S. 1962. *The structure of scientific revolutions.* Chicago: University of Chicago Press.

Labov, W., and Robins, C. 1969. A note on the relation of reading failure to peer-group status in urban ghettos. *Teachers' College Record,* 70: 395-405.

Landis, D.; Hayman, K. L.; and Hall, W. S. 1971. Multidimensional analysis procedures for measuring self-concept in poverty area classrooms. *Journal of Educational Psychology,* 62: 95-103.

LaPiere, R. T. 1936. Type-rationalizations and group antipathy. *Social Forces,* 15: 232-237.

Lester, J. 1968. *Look out Whitey! Black power's gon' get your mama!* New York: Grove Press.

Levin, J. 1968. Three-mode factor analysis. *Psychological Bulletin,* 64: 442-452.

Levi-Schoen, A. 1964. *L'image d'autrui chez l'enfant.* Paris: Presses Universitaires de France.

Lewis, O. 1959. *Five families: Mexican case studies in the culture of poverty.* New York: Basic Books.

———. 1960. *Tepoztlan: Village in Mexico.* New York: Holt.

———. 1961. *The children of Sanchez.* New York: Random House.

———. 1966. The culture of poverty. *Scientific American,* 215: 4, 19-25.

Liebow, E. 1967. *Tally's corner: A study of Negro streetcorner men.* Boston: Little, Brown.

Linton, R. 1936. *The study of man.* New York: Appleton-Century-Crofts.

Lomax, A., and Berkowitz, N. 1972. The evolutionary taxonomy of culture. *Science,* 177: 228-239.

Long, B. H., and Henderson, E. H. 1968. Self-social concepts of disadvantaged school beginners. *Journal of Genetic Psychology,* 113: 41-51.

McNamara, T. C.; Ayrer, J. E.; and Farber, I. J. 1972. Development of semantic differential scales for use with inner-city pupils. Paper presented at the American Educational Research Association, Chicago.

Maruyama, M. 1968. Trans-social rapport through prison inmates. *Annales Internationales de Criminologie,* 7: 19-46.

———. 1969. The ghetto logic. Mimeo.

Miller, K. S., and Dreger, R. M. 1973. *Comparative studies of blacks and whites in the United States.* New York: Seminar Press.

Miller, W. B. 1958. Lower class culture as a generating milieu of gang delinquency. *Journal of Social Issues,* 14: 5-19.

Mitchell, T.; Dossett, D. L.; Fiedler, F. E.; and Triandis, H. C. 1972. Culture training: Validation evidence for the culture assimilator. *International Journal of Psychology,* 7: 97-104.

Morris, C. W. 1946. *Signs, language, and behavior.* Englewood Cliffs, N.J.: Prentice-Hall.

Myrdal, G. 1944. *An American dilemma.* New York: Harper and Bros.

National Institute of Mental Health. 1972. *Bibliography on racism.* DHEW Publication no. (HSM) 73-9012.

Ogden, C. K., and Richards, I. A. 1949. *The meaning of meaning.* London: Rutledge and Kegan Paul.

Osgood, C. E. 1971. Exploration in semantic space: A personal diary. *Journal of Social Issues,* 27: 5-64.

———. 1972. The nature and measurement of meaning. In J. G. Snider and C. E. Osgood, eds., *Semantic differential technique.* Chicago: Aldine-Atherton. Pp. 3-41.

Osgood, C. E., and Suci, G. J. 1955. Factor analysis of meaning. *Journal of Experimental Psychology,* 50: 325-338.

Osgood, C. E.; Suci, G. J.; and Tannenbaum, P. H. 1957. *The measurement of meaning.* Urbana: University of Illinois Press.

Pettigrew, T. F. 1964. *A profile of the Negro American.* Princeton, N.J.: Van Nostrand.

Pinto, P. R., and Buchmeier, J. O. 1973. Problems and issues in the employment of minority, disadvantaged and female groups: An annotated bibliography. Bulletin 59. Minneapolis: Industrial Relations Center, University of Minnesota.

Purcell, T. V., and Cavanagh, G. F. 1972. *Blacks in the industrial world.* New York: Free Press.

Rodman, H. 1963. The lower class value stretch. *Social Forces,* 42: 205-215.

Rose, A. 1948. *The Negro in America.* Boston: Beacon Press.

Rosen, H. 1969. Personal communication.

Ross, J. C., and Wheeler, R. H. 1971. *Black belonging.* Westport, Conn.: Greenwood Publishing Corp.

Rotter, J. B. 1966. Generalized expectancies for internal versus external control of reinforcement. *Psychological Monograph,* vol. 80, no. 1 (whole no. 609).

Ruthledge, A. L., and Gass, G. Z. 1967. *Nineteen Negro men.* San Francisco: Jossey-Bass.

Sampson, E. C. 1969. Studies of status congruence. In L. Berkowitz, ed., *Advances in experimental social psychology.* New York: Academic Press. Pp. 225-270.

Sarbin, T. R. 1954. Role theory. In G. Lindzey and E. Aronson, eds., *Handbook of social psychology.* 1st ed. Reading, Mass.: Addison-Wesley. Pp. 223-258.

Sarbin, T. R., and Allen, V. L. 1968. Role theory. In G. Lindzey and E. Aronson, eds., *Handbook of social psychology.* 2nd ed. Reading, Mass.: Addison-Wesley. Pp. 488-568.

Schuman, H. 1966. Social change and the validity of regional stereotypes in East Pakistan. *Sociometry,* 29: 428-440.

Shielch, A. A., and Miller, P. A. 1971. Investigation of some variables influencing stereotyping in interpersonal perception. *Journal of Psychology,* 78: 213-216.

Stewart, W. A. 1969. On the use of Negro dialect in the teaching of reading. In J. C. Baratz and R. W. Shuy, eds., *Teaching black children to read*. Washington, D.C.: Center for Applied Linguistics. Pp. 156-219.

Suci, G. J. 1960. A comparison of semantic structures in American Southwest culture groups. *Journal of Abnormal and Social Psychology*, 62: 25-30.

Suttles, G. D. 1968. *The social order of the slum: Ethnicity and territory in the inner city*. Chicago: University of Chicago Press.

Taylor, D. A. 1974. Should we integrate organizations? As a black sees it. In H. L. Fromkin and J. J. Sherwood, eds., *Integrating the organization: A social psychological analysis*. Glencoe, Ill.: Free Press. In press.

Triandis, H. C. 1960. A comparative factorial analysis of job semantic structures of managers and workers. *Journal of Applied Psychology*, 44: 297-302.

———. 1964a. Cultural influences upon cognitive processes. In L. Berkowitz, ed., *Advances in experimental social psychology*. New York: Academic Press. Pp. 1-48.

———. 1964b. Exploratory factor analyses of the behavioral component of social attitudes. *Journal of Abnormal and Social Psychology*, 68: 420-430.

———. 1967. Towards an analysis of the components of interpersonal attitudes. In C. and M. Sherif, eds., *Attitudes, ego involvement and change*. New York: John Wiley. Pp. 227-270.

———. 1972. The impact of social change on attitudes. In B. King and E. McGinnies, eds., *Attitudes, conflict and social change*. New York: Academic Press. Pp. 127-137.

———. 1975a. Culture training, cognitive complexity, and interpersonal attitudes. In R. W. Brislin, S. Bochner, and W. J. Lonner, eds., *Cross-cultural perspectives on learning*. New York: Halsted/Wiley. Pp. 39-77.

———. 1975b. Social psychology and cultural analysis. *Journal for the Theory of Social Behavior,* 5:81-106.

Triandis, H. C.; Davis, E. E.; and Takezawa, S. I. 1965. Some determinants of social distance among American, German and Japanese students. *Journal of Personality and Social Psychology*, 2: 540-551.

Triandis, H. C.; Feldman, J.; and Harvey, W. 1970. Person perception among black and white adolescents and the hardcore unemployed. Tech. Rep. no. 5, SRS no. RD 2841-G. Urbana: Department of Psychology, University of Illinois.

———. 1971a. Role perceptions among black and white adolescents and the hardcore unemployed. Tech. Rep. no. 6, SRS no. RD 2841-G. Urbana: Department of Psychology, University of Illinois.

———. 1971b. Job perceptions among black and white adolescents and the hardcore unemployed. Tech. Rep. no. 7, SRS no. RD 2841-G. Urbana: Department of Psychology, University of Illinois.

―――. 1971c. The perceptions of implicative relationships among black and white adolescents and the hardcore unemployed. Tech. Rep. no. 8, SRS no. RD 2841-G. Urbana: Department of Psychology, University of Illinois.

Triandis, H. C.; McGuire, H.; Saral, T.; Yang, K.; Loh, W.; and Vassiliou, V. 1972. A cross-cultural study of role perceptions. In H. C. Triandis et al., eds., *The analysis of subjective culture.* New York: John Wiley. Pp. 263-298.

Triandis, H. C., and Malpass, R. S. 1970. Field guide for the study of aspects of subjective culture. Tech. Rep. no. 4, SRS no. RD-2841-G. Urbana: Department of Psychology, University of Illinois.

―――. 1971. Studies of black and white interaction in job settings. *Journal of Applied Social Psychology,* 1: 101-117.

Triandis, H. C., and Osgood, C. E. 1958. A comparative factorial analysis of semantic structures of Greek and American college students. *Journal of Abnormal and Social Psychology,* 57: 187-196.

Triandis, H. C., and Triandis, L. M. 1960. Race, social class, religion and nationality as determinants of social distance. *Journal of Abnormal and Social Psychology,* 61: 110-118.

―――. 1962. A cross-cultural study of social distance. *Psychological Monograph,* vol. 76, no. 21 (whole no. 540).

―――. 1965. Some studies of social distance. In I. D. Steiner and M. Fishbein, eds., *Recent studies in social psychology.* New York: Holt. Pp. 207-217.

Triandis, H. C., and Vassiliou, V. 1967a. Frequency of contact and stereotyping. *Journal of Personality and Social Psychology,* 7: 316-328.

―――. 1967b. A comparative analysis of subjective culture. Tech. Rep. no. 55. Urbana: Department of Psychology, University of Illinois.

Triandis, H. C.; Vassiliou, V.; and Nassiakou, M. 1968. Three cross-cultural studies of subjective culture. *Journal of Personality and Social Psychology,* 8 (4, pt. 2): 1-42.

Triandis, H. C.; Vassiliou, V.; Vassiliou, G.; Tanaka, Y.; and Shanmugam, A. 1972. *The analysis of subjective culture.* New York: John Wiley.

Triandis, H. C.; Weldon, D. E.; and Feldman, J. 1972. Black and white hardcore and middle class subjective cultures: A cross-validation. Tech. Rep. no. 14, SRS no. 15-P-55175/5. Urbana: Department of Psychology, University of Illinois.

―――. 1974. Level of abstraction of disagreements as a determinant of interpersonal perception. *Journal of Cross-Cultural Psychology,* 5: 59-79.

Tucker, L. R. 1966. Some mathematical notes on three-mode factor analysis. *Psychometrika,* 31: 279-311.

Valentine, C. A. 1968. *Culture and poverty: Critique and counter-proposals.* Chicago: University of Chicago Press.

Walster, E.; Berscheid, E.; and Walster, W. 1973. New directions in equity theory. *Journal of Personality and Social Psychology,* 25: 151-176.

Werner, O., and Campbell, D. T. 1970. Translating, working through interpreters and the problem of decentering. In R. Naroll and R. Cohen, eds., *A handbook of method in cultural anthropology.* New York: American Museum of Natural History. Pp. 398-420.

White, W. F., and Richmond, B. O. 1970. Perception of self and of peers by economically deprived black and advantaged white fifth graders. *Perceptual and Motor Skills,* 30: 533-534.

Wight, A. R. 1969. *Cross-cultural training: A draft handbook.* Estes Park, Colo.: Center for Research and Education.

Wilcox, R. C. 1971. *The psychological consequences of being a black American.* New York: John Wiley.

Williams, J. E. 1964. Connotations of color names among Negroes and Caucasians. *Perceptual and Motor Skills,* 18: 721-731.

————. 1969. Individual differences in color-name connotations as related to measures of racial attitude. *Perceptual and Motor Skills,* 29: 383-386.

Williams, J. E., and Roberson, J. K. 1967. A method for assessing racial attitudes in preschool children. *Educational and Psychological Measurement,* 27: 671-689.

Williams, J. E.; Tucker, R. D.; and Dunham, F. Y. 1971. Changes in the connotations of color names among Negroes and Caucasians, 1963-1969. *Journal of Personality and Social Psychology,* 19: 222-228.

Williams, W. S. 1971. A semantic differential study of the meaning of personality test items to children from different socio-economic groups. *Journal of Psychology,* 79: 179-188.

————. 1972. A study of the use of the semantic differential by fifth grade children from different socio-economic groups. *Journal of Psychology,* 81: 343-350.

Author Index

Subject Index